LEAD With Confidence

Using Common Sense

Dr. Roy W. Harris

ISBN 978-0-9972816-0-6
Soft cover

This book was printed in the United States of America.

To order additional copies of this book, contact:

Dr. Roy W. Harris
906 Castle Heights Ave.
Lebanon, Tennessee 37087
roy@royharris.info
615-351-1425

Order Online
@
www.amazon.com

Table of Contents

Table of Contents (continued)

INTRODUCTION

I'm sure you've heard the expression "*he's or she's a born* leader or possibly *leaders are made not born"*. Well, which is it? Some people seem to be born with a God-given ability to lead others.

While sometimes it seems the most unlikely people develop into exceptional leaders. The truth may be somewhere in between. Good leadership probably requires some of both.

There are certain personality traits which seem to be present in successful leaders, but good leadership also requires knowledge, experience, and wisdom.

There's a plethora of available leadership resources in the modern world with a variety of approaches to leadership. So why offer another one? What can this author offer that is not already readily available?

The author's purpose in penning the words, which follow, is to provide a practical approach to leadership that rookie and veteran leaders alike can use every day in the office.

The book deals with *decision making, second guessing past decisions, relationship building, leadership discernment, receiving and giving criticism, communication, delegating responsibility, admonishing or disciplining, and conducting business meetings, and more.*

The book really is two-books in one. The author wrote the original 12 Chapters on leadership then complimented them by developing a Study Guide as an aid to help the reader better grasp the principles found in these pages. The Study Guide is divided into 12 sections and handily located between chapters.

Is the author qualified to offer common sense suggestions on leadership? At age 16 he began working at Burger Chef starting at that bottom of the employee cycle.

His first leadership role began a year later at age 17 when he was selected by the owner to manage the night shift. Responsibilities included running the night shift, planning the employee work schedule, handling thousands of dollars and managing up to eight employees at a time.

The author led four full-time churches, two of which had Christian schools. He oversaw seven areas at Welch College as Vice President for Institutional Advancement and the entire student body as Dean of Students.

He has overseen up to 20 employees at a time. He also filled a number of denominational leadership roles. He was elected to two terms as President of the Pi Gamma Chi Society (his college fraternity).

He served as moderator or assistant of the Pamlico Association (NC) South Georgia Association (GA) and the Southern Quarterly Association (TN). He served as assistant Moderator then Moderator of the North Carolina Association of Free Will Baptists (approximately 185 churches) at age 33.

He served as Chairman of Ordaining Councils in the Pamlico & Blue Ridge Associations (NC) and the South Georgia Association (GA). He coordinated the 2007 Free Will Baptist National convention in Little Rock, AR, with approximately 6,000 in attendance. He also coordinated the National Leadership Conference in Nashville, TN. He is high demand as a conference and retreat speaker, having spoken in 38 American States, Europe, Israel, and Africa.

Roy is a writer, journalist, and published author. He presently serves as Moderator of Tennessee's Cumberland Association (61 churches).

There are a number of directions one could take approaching leadership. The *LEAD With Confidence principles* in this book reflect lessons learned and a proven leadership style developed by the writer through 40-plus years of experience gained while serving in a variety of leadership roles and managing budgets up to and exceeding $1,000,000.

Both novice and veteran leaders alike can benefit from the sound, common sense approach to leadership tucked away in these pages.

R
M
H

Chapter 1

Leading from the Grease Trap

Lead By Example

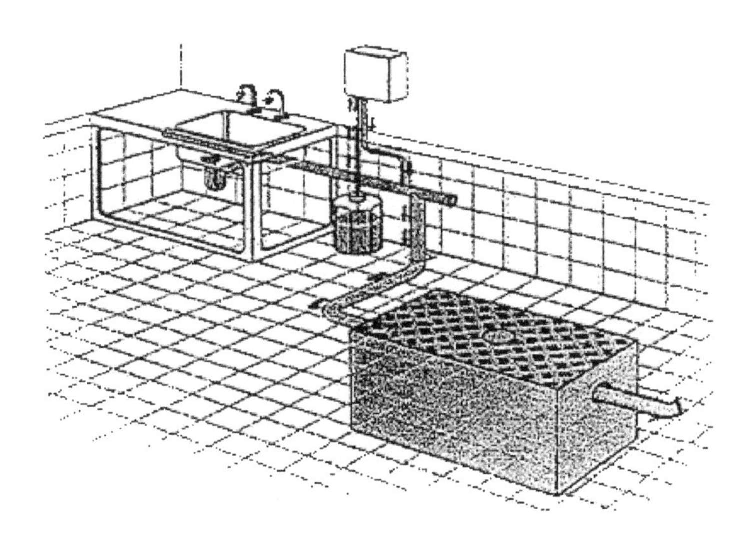

Typical Grease Trap found in many restaurants.

Leading from the Grease Trap.

The dirtiest job at Burger Chef was cleaning the grease trap. All floor drains in the building, fry cutting/washing sinks, and triple sinks drained directly through the grease trap.

The newest rookie employee had the

distinct honor of dipping captured hardened yellow, dark green and black grease from the trap and washing the catch plates.

I've never forgotten my first week on the job and how I felt on my hands and knees in my clean white starched uniform dipping the smelly, nasty, grease from that trap. The manager sat in a chair beside the trap instructing my every move.

Within a year the night manager died unexpectedly, and the owner promoted me to manage the night shift. The first time the trap needed cleaning under my tenure as manager, I made a change in the process.

Word circulated among the employees that the grease trap would be cleaned later in the shift. They began to paint a dire disgusting picture to the latest hire for the nasty job that lay ahead of him.

It was late in the shift when we began cleaning the trap. Instead of following the traditional practice of rolling the manager's office chair next to the trap and supervising the nasty job that was to follow, I got down on my hands and knees beside the newest rookie employee, and we cleaned the trap together. Employees filtered from the front and back serving lines to watch the rookie wade knee deep into the muck and mire.

Why did I choose to help the young man clean the trap? I wanted to send a message that we were a team and that we all would work together to get the job done.

I wanted them to understand that I was willing to get my hands dirty and would be right there with them through the good, the bad, and even the ugly. I also wanted to imprint on their minds that scene so when they were asked to do parts of the job they'd rather not do, they might remember that the boss was willing and did the worst job.

Leading by *example* is contagious and encourages *loyalty* and *morale*. The Encarta Dictionary defines the word *example* as *a person, action or thing taken as a model to be copied*.

Leading by example requires the leader to model the work ethic he wants to see produced in the employees or volunteers under his direction. He cannot be *all things to all people*, but he can communicate by example the bar he has set for work expectations.

He should strive to make sure he adheres to the same standards and expectations he communicated to those he leads. He should arrive at work early, pitch in at peek high pressure times, be willing to work overtime when necessary and endure the same hardships he expects from those he leads.

Attempting to lead from the ivory tower of arrogance, condescension and perceived position entitlement will result in disconnect between leaders and those they lead. It creates a *us versus them* mentality. It lowers morale and smothers any hope of encouraging loyalty to the leader or the organization.

If the leader has to repeatedly *show them who's boss,* then he probably has not modeled well who is the boss to the employees or volunteers. If I am to lead, I am only as good as those who work with me.

As that great Mayberry philosopher Deputy Barney Fife once said; *we are all in this man hunt together.* The attitude of *us versus them* must be replaced with only *us*. A personal approach adopted in my first management position has served as steady guide through all the leadership roles that followed.

Those whom I lead *do not* work *for me* but *with me*. I've conveyed that publically and privately. If the leader constantly reminds others that they work for him, then his leadership role becomes more difficult.

Instead of leading others, many times he finds himself in the role of being forced to drive or push them. If you are a driver rather than a leader, you'll find yourself acting like the man who tried to drive a herd of cats.

You'll do like he did, spend your time chasing individual cats rather than leading the whole herd. This lowers morale and will probably result in less loyalty from employees or volunteers, resulting in a lack of willingness to sacrifice or go the extra mile.

Defining a clear sense of direction and expectations by the leader and serving as an example by coming alongside those being led creates camaraderie and a willingness to follow. Followers will be loyal to those in whom they believe.

STUDY GUIDE

Chapter 1 Leading from the Grease Trap

1. What two reasons did author give for choosing to help clean the grease trap__________________________________

____

____

____

____

2. Leading by example elevates ________________ and _________________.

3. Leading by example requires the leader to _________ the ______ _______ he wants see reproduced in those under his direction.

4. Leaders should strive to adhere to the same ____________ and _______________ he expects from his employees or volunteers.

5. Attempting to lead from a perceived position of being entitled will lead to a __________________ between leaders and those they lead.

6. Leading from an ivory tower of arrogance and condescension leads to an _____ verses ____________ mentality.

7. This attitude lowers ________ and smothers any hope of elevating ________.

8. What has the leader who must show them whose boss failed to do?

____

____

9. A good approach to leadership is to say; those I lead do not work ____ me but ______me.

10. Creating camaraderie and willingness to follow requires the leader to;

a. Define a clear sense of ___________ and ______________ by the leader.

b. Serving as an ___________ by ________ ____________ those being led.

11. Followers will be ____________ to those whom they ____________in.

R
M
H

Chapter 2

Count the Cost

Make the Hard Decisions

2013 Ahoskie, NC, Town Council

Count the Cost.

How do you determine the right course of action to take or which side of an issue to choose? Decision making is not only an everyday part of leadership, but often multiple times a day requirement. The leader is called upon to provide direction on a myriad of organizational questions.

Shortly after settling into my first pastorate, I visited the city hall in our small town and introduced myself to the mayor and city councilman. Fast forward a couple of years. Our church had built a new educational wing complete with a huge fellowship hall. Our daycare had expanded into a full-blown Christian school. Our church was becoming known as a leader in the community.

I was working in my office late one morning when my secretary patched a call through to me. The voice on the other end was one my church members who had a relative who was employed by the city.

The church member informed me that the mayor and town council would be meeting in about an hour to discuss and probably grant a formal request for a license to sell alcohol in a soon to open restaurant which would be located near the church.

State law prohibited the sale of alcohol within 300 feet of a school. The proposed restaurant would be located right on the legal line from our church and school.

There had not been any publicity about alcohol being sold at the restaurant, and the influential, prominent business person who owned it had worked below the radar to secure the license.

The restaurant actually would be nothing more than a bar where a little food would be served. After weighing the pros and cons of the issue, I felt it was in the best interest of the school and church to oppose the granting of the license. The mayor and council members were already in the council chambers when I walked through the door and took a seat near the entrance. I'm sure the mayor was surprised to see me, and I was the only person in the gallery.

In a few minutes the matter of the

license to sell alcohol came up. I asked permission from the mayor to address the council. A councilman who I found out later was close friend of the bar owner objected to me speaking, indicating that I had no standing since I was not a member of the council.

Fortunately for me, there was a reporter for the hometown newspaper taking very good notes of all that was taking place. I looked at the mayor and the mayor was looking at the reporter.

He and I both could see the headlines in tomorrow's newspaper; *Mayor and Council refuse local pastor opportunity to speak.* Our church had become well known in the community, and I had become somewhat known because I spoke six days a week on the local radio station at their request and at no expense to me.

The mayor quickly overruled the councilman and said something to the effect;

there is no harm in allowing Reverend Harris to speak. I didn't think I could convince the council to deny the request for the license, but I believed there should at least be opportunity for input from the community.

So when given the opportunity to speak, I explained that the community had been blindsided by this whole matter and it might appear to some that it had intentionally been done in a way to slip it through.

My recommendation to the council was to postpone the consideration of the matter for two weeks, schedule the hearing in the evening rather than mid-day so those who work could attend, publicize the hearing in the local newspaper, and allow the community to attend and share their feelings on the matter. The council voted unanimously *minus one* to reschedule the hearing for two weeks later. I'll share the outcome of the meeting later in this chapter.

Two questions, if asked and answered by leaders, may serve as a helpful guide in determining courses of action. The first thing to ask is; *what is there to be gained and what could be lost*?

Determining the value of both may help provide a sense of direction. If the cost is more than the benefit, then *no* is the answer. If the benefit far outweighs the possible cost, then the answer is *yes*.

When the decision was made to openly confront the mayor and town council, I knew there would be a cost. I had to weigh what was at stake. It was a matter of principle with me personally but even more importantly; it was a matter of importance for the church and the school.

It might cost the disapproval of a few government officials, but in the end it might reinforce the respect of my church family for me, gain the respect of both the Christian community and the community at large. I later learned we had gained the respect of the mayor and most of the council members through the process.

The issue was approached in a businesslike manner, and I tried to conduct myself as a gentleman by showing proper respect for those in authority. Much more would have been lost if we had not chosen to confront the issue. More could be gained by moving forward than would have been lost by not taking our stand.

The second thing one should ask when trying to determine the right course of action to take or which side of an issue to choose; *is the issue worth losing a relationship over*? Some issues are! The key is understanding how to catalog the issues in your mind.

Most controversial issues that leaders deal with will logically fit in one of two categories.

The first category is that of morals, ethics, or biblical principles. If the decision to be made has to do with dealing with a matter of morality, then one must risk the loss of one or more relationships if necessary. This is not easy, because it calls for direct face-to-face encounters with people you care deeply about. But it must be done.

If the issue is in response to unethical behavior, then the issue must take precedence over the relationship. Unethical conduct must be addressed. One example would be occasions of proven disloyalty to you as the leader. This is unethical and must be dealt with.

The number one characteristic above talent, ability, and competence to me as a leader was always loyalty. I expected those who worked under my leadership to be loyal and supportive.

Making a decision based on biblical

principle is one of the easiest to discern. If the bible says do or not do, then that settles the matter and let the chips fall where they may. The issue is worth the unfortunate sacrifice of a relationship if it involves morals, ethics, or biblical principles

The second category is preference, choice, or a simple matter of opinion. Some things are just not worth losing relationships over! If should not always be *my way or the highway* for the leader. If a decision or proposed action could harm a relationship and it boils down to a matter of opinion, sometimes the better part of valor is to find a way to compromise or choose no action at all.

One situation comes to mind. I was serving as Dean of Students and reported directly to the president of Welch College. I made a decision that the president did not fully agree with.

I learned a great lesson by watching how

he handled me and the situation. He said something like; *Roy, I probably would not have handled it exactly like you did, but you are much closer to it than I am. I trust your decision because I trust you.*

He could have overruled me pointing out why his opinion was the right one. If he'd done that, I probably would have second-guessed other decisions. It might have made me defensive and produced a reluctance to share more than I absolutely had to with him in the future.

Instead, he recognized the value of our working relationship and chose not to chance damaging it because he had a different opinion or preference and did not belittle mine or force me to change it.

When confronted with a decision or action to be taken, ask the important questions. If I choose to take this action or make this decision, what is there to be gained and what might be lost by my organization and me?

After you carefully weigh the value of each, go with your heartfelt instinct and make the decision, which seems to benefit the organization the most. If more will be gained than what might possibly be lost, then you have your answer.

Determine if the matter involves morals, ethics, or biblical principle or is it simply a matter of preference, choice, or opinion? Morality, ethics, and biblical principle demand a strong stand and may require the sacrifice of some relationships.

Prayer and careful consideration should factor heavily in deciding on courses of actions that could cost relationships. Failure to take the strong stand necessary may cause the unraveling of the moral fiber of the organization and also conflict with personal conscience in the leader and his credibility with those he leads. It will also result in lower morale.

If the course of action or decision is only a matter of preference, choice or opinion, then weigh carefully the impact it may have on the organization. If it will not make that much difference one way or the other, do not risk injuring relations with employees or volunteer workers simply because you have a different opinion. Much credibility can be spent with little return on courses of actions which may work fine either way.

Allow those whom you lead to be creative. They may surprise you with innovative ideas and proposed courses of action that will move the organization or church forward. Do not kid yourself by thinking your ideas are always the best; be flexible! My way or the highway mentality by the leader will engender feelings of inadequacy and paranoia in those he leads. It is a proven morale killer.

What about the alcohol and the restaurant? Two weeks later the town council convened to hear the opinions of the community on the proposed liquor license for the Brown Bag Restaurant.

The council chamber was packed and overflowing. Fifteen people spoke in opposition and only one (the business man who wanted the license) spoke in favor. The council voted, and the proposal failed. The license was denied.

I wish I could say that was the end of the story, but the state of North Carolina overruled the city and granted the license. We needed a good steak house in our town, and I asked our church family to begin praying specifically for something.

I asked that we pray and trust the Lord to remove the Brown Bag Restaurant and replace it with a Golden Corral by this same time next year. We prayed. I know it is hard to believe, but exactly one year later to the week, the Brown Bag was gone and a new Golden Corral Restaurant opened its doors at that same location.

STUDY GUIDE

Chapter 2 Count the Cost

1. __________ making is not only an everyday part of leadership but often many times a day _________________.

2. There are two questions which may serve as a helpful __________ in determining ______________ of actions.

3. What is the first question?

   ____

   ____

   ____

4. If the ________ is more than the __________,

then no is the answer.

5. If the __________ far outweighs the possible ______ then the answer is yes.

6. Issues should be approached in a ______________ manner showing proper __________ for those in authority.

7. What is the second thing a leader should ask when trying to determine the right course of action to take

____

____

____

____

8. Are some issues worth losing relationships

over? Yes No If yes, name one

____

____

____

____

____

9. Controversial issues usually fall into how many categories? _________

10. The first category is _______, ________, or _________ ___________.

11. Confrontation on these type issues calls for a face-to-face ___________.

12. __________ behavior may take ___________ over relationships and must be addressed.

13. What is one example of unethical behavior that must be dealt with? ________________

____

____

____

14. What characteristic stands above talent and ability in what the leader expects from those who serve under him?

____

15. Decisions based on _________________ _________ are the easiest to discern.

16. The second category controversial issues fall into is _________, ________ or a simple

matter of ___________.

17. Sometimes the better part of valor is to find a way to __________________ or _______ _________ it at all.

18. When confronted with important decisions, ask the _________ __________.

19. Go with your heartfelt _________and make the decision which seems to _________ the organization the most

20. Allow those you lead to be _____________.

R
M
H

Chapter 3

Aim Before Firing

Don't Jump to Conclusions

Aim before firing.

I recently heard a true story about a poor homeless man who was found dead in a small town. The town council had an agreement with the local funeral home to cover the cost of a cheap graveside service and a plot in the pauper's cemetery.

The funeral director arranged for a young man to play a few songs at the graveside and a local minister to say a few words. Here is the young man's recounting of that occasion in his own words.

> *As a guitarist, I play many gigs. Recently I was asked by a funeral director to play at a graveside service for a homeless man. He had no family or friends, so the service was to be at a pauper's cemetery in the back country. As I was not familiar with the backwoods, I got lost.*
>
> *I finally arrived an hour late and saw the funeral guy had evidently gone and the hearse was nowhere in sight. There were only the diggers and crew left and they were eating lunch.*
>
> *I felt badly and apologized to the men for being late. I went to the side of the grave and looked down and the vault lid was already in*

place. I didn't know what else to do, so I started to play.

The workers put down their lunches and began to gather around. I played out my heart and soul for this man with no family and friends. I played like I've never played before for this homeless man.

And as I played 'Amazing Grace,' the workers began to weep. They wept, I wept, we all wept together. When I finished I packed up my guitar and started for my car. Though my head hung low, my heart was full.

As I opened the door to my car, I heard one of the workers say, "I never seen nothin' like that before and I've been putting in septic tanks for twenty years."

Apparently, I'm still lost he said…

The guitarist had completely misread the situation. He understood the hole in the ground with a concrete box to be a grave when in reality it was a septic tank. His thinking was clouded by his emotions and what he expected to find.

There were similarities between a grave and the septic tank hole. They both were holes in the ground. They both had concrete boxes in them. They both had concrete lids. They both had workers off to the side who would replace the dirt in the hole. But a simple examining of the facts would have revealed what the hole in the ground was really for.

Leaders can make the same mistake. They must be cautious when reading situations. What appears to be one thing after hearing one person's recounting might be the same, slightly different, or altogether different when all the facts are known.

Gathering accurate information is the key to understanding situations. Accurately understanding situations is absolutely necessary if leaders are to make good decisions and take appropriate courses of action.

How can one acquire the information necessary to accurately understand the situation at hand? There is not a magic formula, but there are a few basic things to remember that can be helpful. Understanding who, what, when and where is a great way to put all the pieces together in most situations. Not necessarily in that order but the way it was just stated is an easy way to remember them.

The first question to ask is WHAT. By asking WHAT first you may get answers to other questions as well. *Can you tell my exactly what is going on or what has happened?* By asking this question first one might be able to gain insight on the *nature, parameter* and *seriousness* of the situation.

The second question to ask, if it was not discovered in the WHAT, is WHEN. Time frame is important for a number of reasons. *Can you tell me when this took place* (*happened)*? If it is a small matter and is *old news,* it may not be worth the time and effort to address it now.

Sometimes resurrecting something that has been and should stay buried does more harm than good. If is a recent small matter that can and should be dealt with, then knowing the WHEN is important.

Serious matters should be dealt with sooner rather than later. Moving quickly reinforces the importance and seriousness of the matter. It is important to address the matter while primary parties are present and memories of the facts are clear.

If the issue is serious and a great deal of time has passed, the leader must discern the best course of action. It may or may not be the best thing to bring it to the forefront. Sometimes even serious things should be left alone. Wisdom and maturity will help the leader decide what he should do.

The third question to ask, if not discovered in the first two, is; WHO. Normally the person relating the incident will name the main players in the situation at hand. It is important to know everyone who is involved.

Asking; *can you tell me each person and how they are involved in this matter* will provide names, faces and personalities that will help immensely. Past incidents, patterns or behavior of individuals may be a factor in the present situation. The present situation may be connected to another situation. Knowing who is involved is essential in knowing how to handle the situation.

The fourth question to, it not discovered in the first three, is; WHERE? This also will normally be discovered as the situation is described by the individual(s) who share it with the leader.

WHERE is crucial becomes the location of the incident or situation can make a difference. If the situation took place within in the confines of the organizational employee/volunteer structure, organizational facilities, or organizational sphere of influence, then the leader may have to address it.

If the incident or situation took place outside the parameters of your organization, then it may be a matter for someone outside in some other organization more directly impacted to take care of. It could involve a legal matter and the authorities may need to be contacted to handle it.

It may involve an employee or volunteer worker but has absolutely nothing to do with your organization or church. Knowing where the incident or situation took place may help dictate how a situation should be handled.

Some Final thoughts

Just as a coin always has two sides, there is usually more than one side to every situation. Gather pertinent information and if possible, step back and think about what you've learned, then make decisions based on what your *gut* tells you. Moving too quickly may result in a making a poor decision.

Some situations should just be left alone. If left alone they will work themselves out. The wise leader will not feel obligated to spend time and resources investigating every situation that comes along.

He should listen to the messengers; tell them he appreciates it being brought to his attention. He should then give it careful consideration and hold off the matter if it is not of the nature that should and must be dealt with. Time may take care of it.

Asking the persons who brought the situation to you what they think should be done about the matter is a good thing. You are able to hear their recommendations and expectations. You will also gain insight into the level of concern and emotion they may have invested in it.

It may also be wise to enlist the council of others before a final decision is made (deacons, trustees, organizational board, president's cabinet and etc. Most situations should be dealt with quietly and confidentially. Some situations may bring criticism to the leader and the organization. It is wise to include those who may be directly impacted in the loop so they are not blindsided if criticism comes.

One final thing... Keep your board, committee, council, or etc. between you and controversy. *Always*, again I say *always* keep them informed and included in decisions or actions which may become controversial. A wise thing to do is present the situation at hand to them and ask for their input.

Offer your suggestion for a course of action and ask what they think of that approach. Enlist their support in advance before the direction is chosen. When the decision or course of action is shared with others, communicate to them that; *we (the board, committee, council or etc. and I) feel that we the best course of action is to……….*

R
M
H

STUDY GUIDE

Chapter 3 Aim Before Firing

1. Leaders must be _______________ when _____________situations.

2. ______________ understanding situations is leaders are going to make good decisions.

3. Understanding ________, ________, _________, and ____________ is a good way to acquire information to accurately determine the situation at hand.

4. By asking the first question _______, you may learn the answers to others as well.

5. Why is it important to ask WHEN?

____

____

____

____

6. When should serious matters be dealt with? Explain____

____

____

7. What is the third question that should be asked and why? _________________

____

____

____

8. _________ is the fourth question to ask? It is crucial because the ___________ where the incident __________ __________ can make a difference.

9. If the incident involves a ___________ matter, the ___________ may need to be contacted.

10. Some situations if left _________ will ________ themselves out.

11. Always keep a board, council or committee between you and ____________.

R
M
H

Chapter 4

I Don't Like It.

Handle Criticism with Dignity

The Author's First Church in Ahoskie, NC

I don't like it.

The final meeting of the building committee a few days before the proposal for the new church addition was to be presented would start in a few minutes. One member had failed to attend any of the previous meetings and was not on my good side.

I felt it might be wise to meet with him before the others arrived to field any questions he might have. I uncapped the tube containing the basic floor plan drawings and rolled them out on my desk fully expecting an impressed committee member to commend the plans for the new building.

I remember asking him *well what do you think*. To my surprise he responded *I don't like it*! Even though the red hair of my childhood had changed to Auburn, I still had plenty of freckles at age 28. I felt a shimmer of anger begin to rise in my brain, It shot through my body, causing a tingling sensation to cross my red face and culminate in very expressive words which escaped though my big mouth.

I blurted out in an aggravated unhappy voice *what's wrong with it*! I was really thinking; you *show up at the last meeting. The other building committee members have spent several hours on this. Now you want to criticize our work?* I was not looking for criticism; I was showing him a courtesy.

He was supposed to be *wowed* by the building and not critical. He responded by saying *the restrooms and the offices are in the wrong place. They are reversed. The offices should be near the front entrance.*

The church had begun a Day Care some years before and, along with needing additional Sunday school rooms and a fellowship hall for our church meals, the church had voted to expand the Day Care into a full blown Christian school.

My eyes shifted from his face back to the floor plan on the desk. He was absolutely right! The offices and the bathrooms needed to be reversed.

I'm not sure why we missed it but we did. A fresh set of eyes had caught what would have been a big mistake that would have been around for decades. Recognizing he was right, we made the changes. I've been back to the church on several occasions, and I often remember as I pass by the restrooms how wise it is to listen to constructive criticism

It is impossible to please all the people all the time. Criticism will come if you do nothing. It will come if you do something. I have always felt that is was better to be criticized for doing something rather than nothing.

How we handle criticism is the key. There is a simple personal approach to criticism I developed many years ago and that has served me well, and it may be a help to you also.

What do you do when you received criticism?

1. Step 1 - ***Listen to it***. First of all, when you are criticized take time to *LISTEN TO THE CRITICISM.* Many times we can't get past the

person doing the criticizing to hear what they are saying. Maybe because of past confrontations or disagreements.

Maybe because they are *on the other side* of an issue. Maybe it is just a matter of personality conflicts. One thing I've learned through the years is that you can not only learn from your friends, but you can also learn from those who might oppose you.

The key is: Looking beyond the messenger long enough to hear his message. Be careful not to slam the door on the message because of preconceived feelings about the messenger.

Attend your mental ear to exactly what is being said. If I hadn't moved past my upset feelings for the messenger, I would never have heard the important message he carried.

2. Step 2 – ***Look at it.*** One should examine the merit of the criticism. Are the facts

accurate? Is the criticism valid? Is there a hidden agenda? Once you have taken time to get past the messenger and hear the message, the next step is to determine if the criticism is valid.

Once I had gotten past the criticizer and honestly looked at the criticism, it became obvious that it was a valid and just criticism. If I had dug in my heels and become rigid on the original plan, I would still be reminded of a bad decision made many years ago each time I return to my first church. If the criticism is accurate, then move on to the next step.

3. Step 3 – ***Learn from it.*** If the criticism has merit, do not allow personal pride or stubbornness to stand in your way. Learn what you can from the criticism. Determine if the situation can be improved or corrected. Define what actions, corrections or adjustments need and can be taken. Man up or woman up and determine to do what needs to be done.

Develop a plan for action and make the changes needed.

4. Step 4 – ***Live above it***. What if the criticism is not valid? There are many situations which come to mind, but I remember one in particular. A church member caught me in the foyer between Sunday school and morning worship service (the worst time for a pastor to hear criticism).

The previous Sunday we had begun a time of fellowship during the opening part of the service. Our auditorium was large and this fellowship time provided an opportunity to shake hands and greet folks from across the building.

It also enabled older folks who could not get around well to be greeted and told they were loved by the rest of the congregation. It was a warm, enjoyable time which took place early in the service.

The church member conveyed in a kind way that he didn't think it was a good idea to have this fellowship time. He expressed his reasons and asked me to consider stopping the fellowship time. Now this was one of the *good guys* who supported me on most decisions and was a great church member.

What should I do? The first thing I did was thank him for the sharing his concern with me. It is always a good idea to thank the person for sharing the criticism. I do not solicit criticism but I'd rather know about one than have it make its way to several others before it reaches me.

The next thing is to make a commitment to look into it. I did not promise anything else. I quietly approached a half-dozen people individually who I thought represented a good cross section of our congregation.

I did not hint of any criticism but simply asked them what they thought of our new morning worship service fellowship time. Their responses were unanimous. Every one of them thought it was the greatest thing that had come along since banana pudding. Well, that may be a stretch but they all liked it and felt it was something our people enjoyed.

I had my answer. After weighing the criticism and giving it a great deal of thought, I determined that the criticism was without merit and the best thing to do was continue with the fellowship. By the way, two pastors and years later during the Sunday morning worship service, the fellowship time still continues.

What should you do? After listening to and looking at criticism and finding it without merit, determine that you will simply *live above it*. Keep doing what you're doing.

What about when you feel it's necessary to give criticism? More will be said in a later chapter and a suggested approach will be given. I want to insert one important thing at addressing it here.

One should give criticism in the way and manner he would prefer to receive it. The Bible admonition to *treat others the way we would like to be treated* is a great way to approach others with criticism.

One should spend time thinking about the matter and choose his time, manner, and words of criticism wisely. The wise leader should also offer possible solutions to those he confronts with criticism. It's not enough to simply tell someone you don't like something. If one's heart is in the right place, he wants to help find solutions for the matters at hand.

Remind yourself again that it would be great if you could please everybody all the time, but that simply is not possible. Do what you believe is right and take the path you've discerned to be the correct one.

Continue your march forward in the kingdom. Remember who you really work for, the Lord Jesus Christ. He is the one to please.

Do you remember the old expression; *if momma is not happy, then no one will be happy*? Well, our goal is to make Jesus happy. If He is happy then everything else will fall into place.

R
M
H

STUDY GUIDE

Chapter 4 I Don't Like It.

RECEIVING CRITICISM

1. It is wise to _________ to criticism.

2. ___________ will come if you do ________ or if you do _____________.

3. What are the 4 steps to take when you receive criticism?

   a. ______________________________

   b. ______________________________

   c. ______________________________

   d. ______________________________

4. Why is it hard to listen to some people's criticism?

   ____

   ____

   ____

   ____

5. Why is important to look beyond the messenger bringing the criticism?

   ____

   ____

   ____

   ____

6. One should look at the __________ of the criticism. What three things should you ask yourself?

   a. ______________________________________

b. ______________________________

c. ______________________________

7. If the criticism has merit, do not allow __________ or ___________ to keep you from learning from it.

8. Determine if the situation can be _____________ or ______________.

9. Define what ________, ___________ or __________ can be taken.

10. Develop a _____ of action and ______ the changes that are needed.

11. What should the leader do if the criticism is not valid?

____

____

____

____

GIVING CRITICISM

1. One should ______ criticism in the _________ he would want to receive it.

2. Choice of the __________, ____________, and words used to criticize should be chosen wisely.

3. The wise leader will ______ possible _________ to those he confronts with criticism.

FINAL THOUGHTS

1. The leader should be reminded that it is not possible to __________ all the people all the __________.

2. When criticism comes.

    a. ________ to it.

    b. ________ at it.

    c. ________ from it.

    d. ________ above it.

3. The leader should ___ what he ____________ is right and take the ______ he has __________ to be the right one.

R
M
H

Chapter 5

Say What?

Communication

The author spoke at a *Living Beyond Grief Conference* at Lakeview Fellowship in Bowling Green, KY.

Say What?

I remember reading a story about a rather old-fashioned lady, who was planning a vacation in Florida. She was quite delicate and elegant with her language.

She emailed a particular campground

and asked for reservations. She wanted to make sure the campground was fully equipped with indoor bathrooms but didn't quite know how to ask about the restroom/bathroom facilities.

She just couldn't bring herself to write the word restroom, commode or toilet in her email. After much thought, she finally came up with the old fashioned term "*Bathroom Commode*," but when she wrote that down, she still thought she was being too forward.

So she started all over again; rewrote the entire email and referred to the Bathroom Commode" simply as the "B.C.". *Does the campground have its own "B.C."* is what she actually wrote?

Well, the campground owner wasn't old fashioned at all, and when he received the email, he couldn't figure out what in the world the lady was talking about. That "B.C." completely stumped him. After worrying about it for several days, he showed the email to other campers, but they couldn't figure out what the lady meant either.

The campground owner finally came to the conclusion that the lady must be asking about the location of the local *Baptist Church*. So he emailed her the following reply:

> *"Dear Madam: I regret very much the delay in answering your email, but I now take pleasure of informing you that the "B.C." is located nine miles north of the camp site and is capable of seating 250 people at one time. I admit it is quite a distance away if you are in the habit of going regularly. But no doubt you will be pleased to know that a great number of people take their lunches along, and make a day of it..... They usually arrive early and stay late.*
>
> *The last time my wife and I went was six years ago, and it was so*

crowded we had to stand up the whole time we were there. It may interest you to know that right now, there is a supper planned to raise money to buy more seats.....They plan to hold the supper in the middle of the B.C., so everyone can discuss this great event together.....It pains me very much, not to be able to go more regularly, but it is surely not for lack of desire on my part....As we grow older, it seems to take more and more effort, particularly in cold weather..... If you decide to come down to the campground, perhaps my wife and I could go with you and your husband the first time... sit with you... and introduce you to all the other folks..... Our community is very friendly and I know you'll enjoy your visit with us.

Good communication is the tether that connects leaders with those they lead. Just like the illustration above, poor communication can result in multitudes of real or perceived issues.

One way to maintain good communication is to schedule regular meetings with those whom one leads. This will provide opportunities for others to keep the leader informed of what is happening.

It also gives opportunity for the leader to hear their successes, concerns, and personal issues. Sometimes just getting something off the chest is enough for some situations. These meetings benefit the leader by giving him opportunity to express appreciation, concerns, and instructions for future actions to those he is leading.

The issues at hand will dictate meeting content and duration. Sometimes they will be dead serious and sometimes they should be light and casual (just catching up). NEVER cancel regularly scheduled individual meetings because you have nothing to talk with that individual about.

He may have something he needs to share with you. Even if neither has anything urgent, just spending a few minutes in casual conversation is good for building personal and working relationships.

These regularly scheduled meetings normally should take place in the leader's office. This location tends to frame the lines of authority and helps the leader control the meeting.

The office door should be closed during these meetings. Meetings with the opposite sex should be done with office door at least cracked but preferably kept wide open. If delicate or confidential matters are to be discussed and the door needs to be closed, then a third person should be invited to attend the meeting.

One more suggestion for leaders about the office door; *do not* keep your office door closed most or all of the time. This communicates to those you labor with that you want to be left alone.

It also conveys a message that you are unapproachable. Those you lead will be hesitant to knock on your door for fear that they are disturbing you. They will feel that whatever you are doing is more important than what they may want to talk with you about. The *closed door policy* will construct an unintentional wall between the leader and those he leads.

Close the office door for confidentiality, times of personal study, private phone calls, when deadlines are pressing, etc. but leave it open as much as reasonably possible. Leaving the door open will provide opportunities for those you lead to just pop in and say hello. They may drop in for a few minutes just to *chew the fat*. But they may have a pressing issue and will be so glad you have a minute to talk with them.

The greatest benefit to the leader is the communication to those he leads that his door is always open to the needs of those who follow his leadership. The leader should want those he leads to feel that he is approachable. Keeping the door open helps communicate this. Keeping the office door open eliminates an obstacle and helps open the door for better communication.

Occasionally, call the employees and tell them you'd like to come to their office or meet in their area of responsibility. Bring their favorite soft drink or a bottle of water. Make it a relaxing meeting with them in their area of service.

This does a couple of things. It lets them know that you know where they labor and what they do. It also communicates that what they do is important. Simply taking time to sit down in their office, shop, etc. will let them know they are valuable in the leader's eyes. This small action will lay one more brick in the building of relationships and maintaining good morale.

These meetings should have a pre-set time limit. The date and time of the next meeting should be set or reaffirmed before the present meeting ends.

There are a number of MEANS we use to communicate with those we lead. How we use those vehicles is important. I'll mention four.

- Face-to-face is always the best choice. The leader needs to choose his words carefully. Equally important is his knowing how the message is being received. Face-to-face communication provides that opportunity. Body language, such as folded arms, changing of facial expressions, restlessness, eye contact, etc., sometimes convey to the leader how the employee or volunteer worker is receiving his message. The leader will also be able to react to what he learns from the body language.

The employee or volunteer worker will also be able to observe the leader in the face-to-face context. He'll see the reaction of the leader as they discuss the issues of the day. Both will better understand each other by not only hearing what the other has to say but observing his behavior when he says it.

- A second vehicle of communication in the 21st century world is email. Email is the modern world's instant version of the pre-technology world's hand-written letter. Email can be a tremendous help to the leader.

When and how should the leader use email to communicate with those he leads? Email is a valuable tool but cannot take the place of the personal, face-to-face touch with people. Many employees and volunteer workers receive email on their phones as well as their computers. Email is useful in communicating general information, requesting information, or making announcements. Others can read the leader's email quickly and respond accordingly. Email should not be used to communicate negative, critical or controversial matters.

Email should be carefully crafted using only words, which have been wisely chosen. Keep in mind that people read and interpret what is written differently sometimes. The wise leader will try to put himself in the place of those who will be reading it.

Read it as though you were the one is receiving it rather than the one who is sending it. One should always remember that email is a lasting written record which can be saved and retrieved at a later time. Spelling and grammar are also important. Misspelled words, using the wrong tense or verb, failing to capitalize appropriate words, using all caps, etc. will cause the intended message to be overshadowed and will convey an unintended message of incompetence or anger on behalf of the sender.

- A third vehicle of communication is the phone. Whether land line or cell phone, the phone can be a valuable tool to the leader for communication. When should the leader use the phone? When information, a short answer to a question, or a quick decision is needed.

The phone can also be used to address matters that are not serious enough to require a face-to-face meeting or the crafting and sending of an email. If at all possible, the phone should not be used to discuss controversial matters or other issues that may require lengthy discussion. If an employee or volunteer worker who calls the leader is angry, the leader should offer to meet with them in person at a mutually agreed upon time and place. It is much better to discuss difficult matters face to face.

- A fourth vehicle of communication for the leader is texting. It took me a while to come around to this one, but it does have value. Especially when the leader is away from the office. Texting saves time. A brief message takes less time than a phone call and sometimes can be just as effective. Messages should be brief and in this context abbreviated words and shortened sentences are appropriate.

There is another important thing to remember about communication. Sometimes you may know more than you should communicate to others. You may receive a complaint about an employee that is not worth sharing with the employee or volunteer worker. Some things are better left unsaid. Repeating them may discourage a worker when nothing will be gained. Some things are better left alone.

Also, when sharing information with others, it is important to know how much information is enough and when to stop before saying too much. Too little information may garner suspicion while too much may lead to more questions. You may undergo criticism and you may be misunderstood, but you cannot always reveal everything you know. This is especially true in public settings. Sometimes you may wish that you could reveal the unpublished details that might present you as the leader in a better light. Carrying this load is part of being a leader.

Communication is like the strands of a spider's web. It should move easily in all directions and flow from to and from the center point of the organization. The leader defines the conduit and communicates by his example.

STUDY GUIDE

Chapter 5 Say What?

1. Good communication is the __________that connects leaders with those they lead.

2. Poor communication can result in __________ or __________ issues.

3. What is one way to maintain good communication?

   ____

   ____

4. What are some positive things which can be gained by this way?

   a. It will provide opportunities for others to keep the leader __________.

b. The leader can hear the __________, __________, and ________ _______ from those he is leading.

c. It gives the leader opportunity to express ____________, ___________, and _______________ for future actions to those he is leading.

d. Sometimes just getting __________ off the _________ is enough for some situations.

5. ___________ cancel a regularly scheduled individual meeting because there are no issues which need talking about.

6. Regularly scheduled meetings should normally take place in the __________ ________.

7. This location tends to ________ the lines of authority.

8. The office _______ should be _________ during these meetings.

9. Meetings with opposite sex should take place with the office _______ at least ________ cracked but preferably _______ __________.

10. Why should the office door not be kept closed all the time?

____

____

____

____

11. When should the office door be closed?

____

____

____

____

12. Occasionally meet with employees or volunteers in their ______ of __________.

13. Why is this important?

____

____

____

14. What are four MEANS of we use to communicate?

    a. ______________________________ is the best choice.

b. ______________________________ is the second vehicle.

c. The third vehicle is ____________________________.

d. _____________ is the fourth vehicle of communication we use.

FINAL THOUGHTS

1. Sometimes the leader will know ________ than he should _____________ to others.

2. Some things are left better _____________. Repeating them may ____________ an employee or volunteer when nothing will be gained.

3. Too ________ information may garner _________ and to _________ information may lead to more questions.

4. The leader may be misunderstood but he ___________ always reveal everything he knows.

5. The leader defines the ___________ of _______________ by his example.

Chapter 6

A Visit with the Sergeant Major

Delegate Responsibility

The Author's 2nd day in the U.S. Army.

A Visit the Sergeant Major.

The day before my 20th birthday I received a personal letter from the president of the United States. The letter was short and to the point. I do not remember the exact words, but I had no trouble understanding them. The letter said something to the effect; *Greetings from the president for the United States. This is to inform you that you are being inducted into the Armed Forces of the United States. You are hereby ordered to report to the post office in Anderson, IN, to travel by bus to the U.S. Army induction center in Indianapolis on September 20th.*

Fast forward one year. I had become a full-blown soldier and fortunate to be part of the headquarters command unit at Fort Leonard Wood, Missouri. A new program was begun by the Army to provide crisis intervention training for officers. The program took place in the building next to the post headquarters command building. I was also fortunate to have been selected by the program commander to assist in the training program.

One morning we received word that The I.G (Inspector General of the Army) would be on Post in a few days to inspect all aspects of Post operations including our facility. My boss assigned me the responsibility of ensuring that our facility was clean, organized, and ready for inspection. He told me to go next door see the post Sergeant Major (the highest ranked Sergeant at Fort Leonard Wood) and request a work detail to assist me.

I was terrified of the post Sergeant Major. I'd received three promotions but the Sergeant Major had been in the Army longer than my entire life. I decided I would just put in extra hours and get ready for the inspection by myself.

My boss arrived the next morning and found me scrubbing our floors in preparation for the inspection. He asked me when the work detail would arrive. I mentioned sheepishly that I had not requested one (the Top Sergeant had the reputation of eating 2nd Lieutenants for breakfast, and I was a lowly enlisted man).

He walked past me into his office. He then did something he'd never done before to me. He usually called me by my first name but I heard; *Specialist, front and center*. I walked into his office. He snapped me to attention. He asked me why I had not secured the work detail from headquarters command.

I fumbled for words but had none. He then told me to go next door and request a work detail and reinforced it by saying; *that is a direct order*. Failure to comply with a direct order could have resulted in my being court-martialed. He commanded; *about face....forward march*. He marched me out of his office and out the front door. Lucky for me he did not follow me out the door.

I went next door and talked with the Top Sergeant. He granted my request, and the work detail arrived at our facility within an hour. We finished the work in a fraction of the time that it would have taken me if I had done all the work alone.

The most important lesson I learned that day was that if you are going to lead, you have to delegate. You must assign tasks to others and let others help you. The reason leaders hire people and recruit volunteers is so more can be accomplished, and in most case it will done better. A leader may be good at many things but he cannot attempt many things by himself and expect to do them well.

My boss delegated me the responsibility of preparing our facilities for the most important inspection we would ever undergo. He laid his credibility on the line. He expected me to get it done and do it right. But he did not expect me to do the bulk of the work alone.

He trusted me to develop a plan, clearly articulate that plan to others, assign individual duties and responsibilities to others, and lead them through the completion of I. G. Inspection preparations.

What is the first step in delegating responsibility? Oddly enough, the first step is *careful selection* of those workers the leader surrounds himself with. Leaders should seek workers who are better than they are in the areas they oversee.

Wise leaders vest gifted, capable people with one up-front qualification requirement – Loyalty. I wanted people who would be loyal to me and to the organization we served. I let them know up front that disloyalty to either was grounds for immediate termination. It's important for those to whom you hand off responsibility to know that they carry with them your credibility and the good name the organization may have taken years to acquire.

A second step in delegating is to *define the parameters*. Developing job descriptions which defined roles, responsibilities, chain of command, etc. may serve as a tool to help accomplish this. Much thought should be given to each position. Thought should also be given on how each position impacts other positions and the boundaries should be clearly established for all positions.

A third step in delegating responsibility is to simply let those you lead *do their work.* You might be able to do a few things even better in a person's area of responsibility than they can, but you must allow them to do their jobs. It's as simple as that. If you are constantly stepping in and doing their work for them, they are of little value to you.

Delegating is *handing off* not hanging on! If you micromanage people and try to keep your hand in the middle of everything, you undermine those who work under you. They feel that you do not have enough confidence in them to allow them to do their jobs. Their creativity will be smothered and there morale dampened. They should always feel that you are a lifeline of support if they need you and not a ball and chain holding them back.

A fourth step in delegating is *expecting results*. When you trust people with responsibility, lend them your personal credibility, allow them to carry the good name of the organization, and sometimes provide financial remuneration, then you have the right to expect them to accomplish the tasks assigned to them.

A good friend of mine Mr. Pat McLaughlin who is the president and CEO of The Timothy Group once said; *never assume that it will be done, because it's not what you expect it's what you inspect that gets results.* When work has been delegated it must be inspected. It's important for leaders to let those they lead know up front that a time of review and inspection will come. It is wise to define clear time frames for task completion and accountability reporting dates. Everyone involved should know what needs to be done, who is going to do it, when it should be completed, and when the final results will be reviewed.

One final step is *praise and recognition* for successful completion of assigned tasks. I can hear someone saying; *if it's their job, they should have done it anyway.* Well, that is true to a point. But it costs the leader very little to let people know he appreciates them and their hard work. It may result in big dividends in future projects.

By the way... we passed the I.G. Inspection with flying colors. I completed my tour of duty and was honorably discharged from the U.S. Army.

I've attached the Letter of Commendation I received from my boss upon my departure. Please note the comments in the last few paragraphs about the facilities.

R
M
H

Copy of the Letter of Commendation the author received at his departure from the U.S. Army.

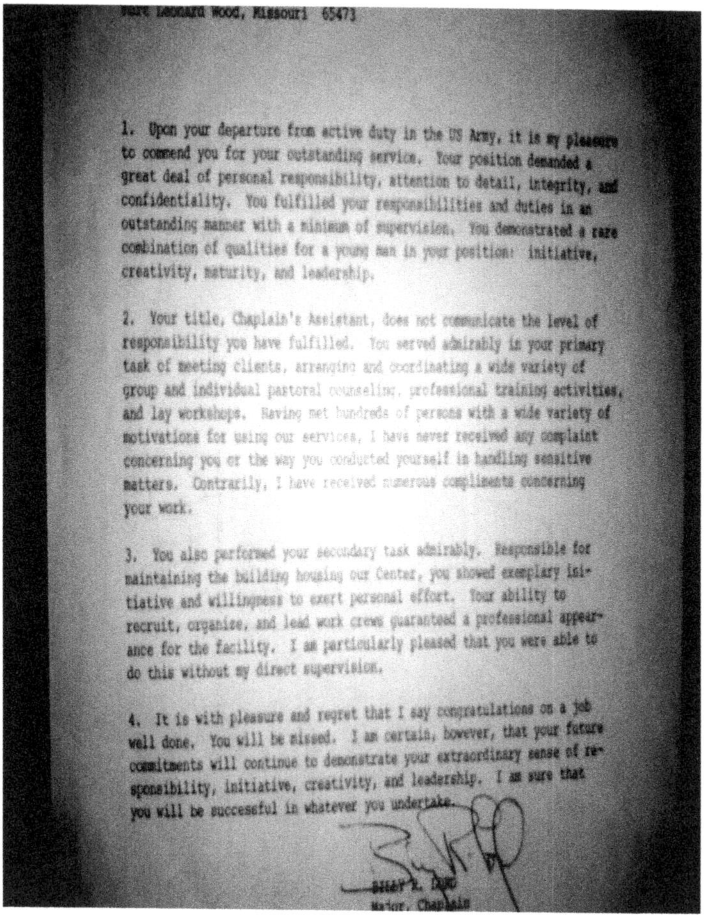

Fort Leonard Wood, Missouri 65473

1. Upon your departure from active duty in the US Army, it is my pleasure to commend you for your outstanding service. Your position demanded a great deal of personal responsibility, attention to detail, integrity, and confidentiality. You fulfilled your responsibilities and duties in an outstanding manner with a minimum of supervision. You demonstrated a rare combination of qualities for a young man in your position: initiative, creativity, maturity, and leadership.

2. Your title, Chaplain's Assistant, does not communicate the level of responsibility you have fulfilled. You served admirably in your primary task of meeting clients, arranging and coordinating a wide variety of group and individual pastoral counseling, professional training activities, and lay workshops. Having met hundreds of persons with a wide variety of motivations for using our services, I have never received any complaint concerning you or the way you conducted yourself in handling sensitive matters. Contrarily, I have received numerous compliments concerning your work.

3. You also performed your secondary task admirably. Responsible for maintaining the building housing our Center, you showed exemplary initiative and willingness to exert personal effort. Your ability to recruit, organize, and lead work crews guaranteed a professional appearance for the facility. I am particularly pleased that you were able to do this without my direct supervision.

4. It is with pleasure and regret that I say congratulations on a job well done. You will be missed. I am certain, however, that your future commitments will continue to demonstrate your extraordinary sense of responsibility, initiative, creativity, and leadership. I am sure that you will be successful in whatever you undertake.

[illegible]
Major, Chaplain

R
M
H

STUDY GUIDE

Chapter 6

A Visit with the Sergeant Major

1. If a leader is to lead, he must learn to ___________.

2. Leaders hire _________ and recruit ____________ so more can be accomplished.

3. What is the first step in delegating responsibility? ______________________ ______________________________________ ____________________________________

4. Leaders should hire people who are _______ than they are in _______ they oversee.

5. What is the most important quality to look for in people you lead? _______

6. It is important for employees and volunteers to remember that delegating entrusts the leader's _____________ and the organization's ________ _______ to their hands. They should act accordingly.

7. The second step in delegating is to __________ ___ ___________.

8. The third step in delegating to let workers ______ ______ ______.

9. Leaders should remember that delegating is ____________ off and not ______________ on.

10. Failure to do this will result in ___________ being smothered and ____________ being dampened.

11. The leader should be a ___________ of support and not a _______ and chain holding back his workers.

12. ________ _________ is the fourth step in delegating.

13. It is not what you ____________ but what you ___________ that will produce results.

14. Work that is delegated must be _____________.

15. Leaders should clearly define time frames for task _____________ and dates when they will be held _______________.

16. Everyone involved should know;

    a. __________ needs to be done.

    b. __________ is going to do it.

    c. __________ it should be completed.

    d. __________ the final results will be reviewed.

17. _________ and ___________ for successful completion of assigned tasks is the final step.

18. It ________ the leader _____ ____ to let people know he appreciates their hard work.

19. It may result in big_________ in future __________.

R
M
H

Chapter 7

The Positive/Negative Approach

Correct, Admonish, and Discipline Others

The Positive/Negative Approach.

Leading requires dealing with those who fail to meet expectations. Confrontation is not easy but failure to address shortcomings will result in repeated offenses and undermine the effectiveness of the organization. Dealing with issues relating to failure in meeting expectations can be some of the most sensitive and difficult issues a leader must face.

I was present in a meeting when our boss began to point out things that, in his opinion, a particular person had done wrong. I looked briefly at the individual on the receiving end and then followed suit with others in the room by shifting my eyes away and looking into infinity.

The countenance of the person receiving the chastisement changed from a happy healthy one to a pale, sad, downtrodden one in a matter of seconds. I watched the blood literally drain from the person's face. The boss clicked off the offenses and then finished the whole thing with a; *but I want you to know that I really appreciate you.*

By this point the compliment was totally lost in the fog of embarrassment and feelings of ridicule that were hanging in the room. This encounter should have taken place in the boss's office. The rest of us should not have witnessed it. In my opinion there is a better approach.

Avoid dealing with negative matters through email, text or telephone. Anything that can be most likely will be misunderstood if it is sent in print. The leader can better read the person he's dealing with if the matter is handled face to face.

It is important to see the body language of the person on the receiving end. Facial expression, crossed arms and legs, nervous shifting around in the chair, lack of eye contact and etc. may indicate the true manner in which the person is receiving what is being sent their way. The leader's body language may also convey to the person on the receiving end the leader's sincerity and displeasure.

The best place to deal with corrective matters is in the office and not in a public place. The setting is more private and confidential. The person will more readily accept correction or criticism in the office of the leader they are following rather than the embarrassment of it happening in front of others.

The office desk is also important. It is a symbol of the leader's position and authority. Sitting behind the desk when admonishing or correcting, will reinforce the roles and remind the person on the receiving end of his personal accountability.

Not what is said, but how it is said can make a huge difference. A good approach to take is to first show genuine appreciation to the individual for recent contributions to the organization. Doing this before bringing up the negative matter frames the conversation in a positive context. Point out some recent thing the person has done well. Make them feel at ease. By doing this first, it will soften the blow of correction that will soon follow.

After complimenting the person and letting him know you appreciate the hard work he has done, how should you bring up the negative matter? There is a simple way to bring up the issue that needs to be addressed. Calling the person by name and saying something like; *Bill, there is something we need to talk about.* Then proceed to share the issue at hand.

It would be wise to give the issue a good bit of thought before the meeting. Maybe even jot down a few simple reminder points you can refer to during the discussion. State the problem in a clear, concise way. After stating the problem or issue, allow the person to respond with his questions, feelings, and side of the story.

It is important to develop a plan to correct the problem. I often ask the individual; *what do you think we should do now?* Many times they will suggest what I have already come to the conclusion should happen. If they say they do not know, I usually say: *I think this is what we probably should do.* I try to make it simple and ask if they understand or if they have any questions.

After dealing with the negative issue, how do you end the meeting? I would suggest rising from your chair and coming around the desk. I usually shake hands with the individual and conclude the meeting looking him in the eye and letting him know how I appreciate him and how important his service is to the church or organization.

After dealing with negative issues, re-affirming the value of people will often leave a good taste in their mouths and a positive frame of mind. Hopefully, this will go a long way toward correcting the matter at hand. Walk the person to the door and leave the door open until he moves completely out of your sight instead of closing it as soon as he passes through it. Closing the door quickly may send a wrong signal that you are glad to get rid of him. By waiting, you signal that both he and his time are important to you.

We've looked at how and where to deal with negative issues in a positive manner. When should you deal with negative issues? Timing is everything! Other chapters provide insight into how to know the right time. I want to address the wrong time. Sometimes people just drop by the office to say hello or *chew the fat.* Unless the matter is urgent and cannot wait, it is usually best to delay confronting the issue until the next visit.

One must remember that leading is also about building. Building strong relationships with those you lead is an essential part of inspiring others to follow. Leaders should seek to create an atmosphere where those they lead not only feel free but want to see their leaders up close.

The worker may have dropped by the office with a need for personal encouragement or job-related advice on an issue in his area of responsibility. To hit him with an; *oh by the way I have an issue with you that we need to talk about* may cause him to become gun shy and prevent him from dropping by in the future. This will hinder the relationship.

This could negatively impact the church or organization because matters that need joint input, strategy, and effort may unintentionally be sacrificed. You can always touch base tomorrow and arrange for another meeting to deal with the issue at hand.

Let me point another thing that it would be wise to remember. How should you give criticism? Offer solutions and not only problems.

STUDY GUIDE

The Positive/Negative Approach

1. Leading requires dealing with those who fail to _______ ____________.
2. Failure to address _______________ will result in __________ __________.
3. Avoid dealing with __________ matters through ______, _____, or _______.
4. Anything that can be most likely will be _____________ if sent in in_______.
5. Why is it important to observe to body language of the person on the receiving end?

   ____

   ____

   ____

   ____

6. Where is the best place and worst place to deal with corrective matters?

   ____

   ______________________Why?____________________

   ____

   ____

   ____

7. Why is the office desk important?

   ____

   ____

   ____

8. Not _________ is said but ________ it is said can make a huge difference.

9. The leader should first show ____________ ____________ for recent contributions to the organization. Why is this important?

____

____

____

10. After complimenting the person, how should the leader bring up the issue which needs addressing?

____

____

____

____

11. It would be wise to ________ down a few simple ____________ points before the meeting.

12. After stating the problem, allow the person to share his ______ _____, ____________ and _______ of the __________.

13. It is important to develop a _____ to correct the ____________.

14. What is a good question to ask the individual in seeking his input in finding a solution to the problem? ____

15. What should the leader do after dealing with issues and at the close of the meeting? ____

16. Why is it important to re-affirm value after dealing with negative issues?

____

____

____

____

17. Why should the leader leave his door open until the person is completely out of his sight?

____

____

____

____

18. __________ is about ______________ relationships.

19. Building strong __________ is an essential part of_______ others to follow.

20. Explain the importance of not bringing up negative issues when individuals stop by just to say hello or *chew the fat.*

____

____

____

____

____

____

Chapter 8

It's Not My Fault

Give Credit – Accept Blame

The picture is of the 100-year-old Dogwood Tree in the yard of the author's 2nd church.

It's not my fault.

I learned much during my first pastorate and now had moved to the opposite end of the state. Our church was doing well. We'd voted to tear down the parsonage and provide funds for the pastor and his family (me) to purchase his own home. That had been accomplished and the front yard looked clean and fresh since its removal. We hired and architect to design a new auditorium, offices, restrooms, etc. The beautiful octagon shaped building was innovative and would serve us well. Things were going well and morale was high. There was still one obstacle yet standing in the way of the new building.

It was about the middle of summer and we were sprucing up the church and grounds in preparation for a big upcoming Sunday. I went to my office for a few minutes in my jeans and t-shirt to attend to a pressing matter while the work continued outside. The weather in the mountains was pleasant year round and this super day was no different. The air conditioning was not on, and my office window was open. My back was turned to the window as I worked at my desk.

There was a monument in the middle of the church front yard. Some people said it had stood in place for over 100 years. It was one of the prettiest Dogwood trees one has ever seen. It was almost magical when in full bloom. But on this day it was about to become a curse.

I heard a voice from the other side of the screen call; *preacher.* I swung my desk chair around and a gentleman on the other side of the screen wanted to talk a minute. He complained about the lower limbs of the Dogwood tree hitting him when he tried to mow under it. He said; *sometime I'm going to come by here and trim that tree so we can mow.*

I agreed that the tree needed trimming, but little did I know what he had in mind. To my horror an hour or so later he walked into my office and said; *preacher, I took care of that tree.* Well, *taking care* is a relevant term and means different things to different people. I stood up, turned around and looked through the window at the Dogwood tree. To my horror the man had butchered it. It went from a proud, healthy looking Dogwood to a sick tree that looked like it had gone through a tornado.

I felt as if the blood was completely draining from my body. I didn't say much to the man, but I dreaded what I might face when the church congregation arrived the next day and observed the major surgery which had occurred. I was not disappointed.

Comments like; *preacher, what in the world did* ***you*** *do to our tree* and *that tree's been here a hundred years and now* ***you've*** *ruined it.* I saw red faces, veins popping out in necks, little old ladies (and big ones too) almost screaming, and grown men raising their voices. I think I saw a few tears filling some eyes as well.

Believe me, that is not the best way to begin a Sunday morning, and you can imagine how spiritual the service was.......not! I went home that afternoon ready to resign. I did not see how I could get past this.

A deacon's meeting had already been scheduled for that afternoon. I had three good men who I trusted and whose support for me was unwavering. We gathered for the meeting in my office. I'd planned to bring up the matter of the Dogwood tree. Before I could, my youngest deacon brought it up first. He asked; *Pastor, have you heard any comments about the tree?* I wasn't sure where he was going with the question, but I recounted what had taken place and told them that I had given permission for the tree to be trimmed.

I was the pastor and the buck stopped with me. I didn't want the fellow who thought he was doing something to help to receive what might have been enough criticism to cause him and his family to leave the church. The deacons had already knew who was responsible. They told me that they appreciated my willingness to take the blame and shield the individual but they felt that the issue would not go away unless something was done.

All three of my deacons were wise men. I respect and appreciate each one to this day. I asked them what they thought I should do. My youngest deacon said; *Pastor, I'd have that tree cut down and gone by church time Wednesday. You'll hear nothing but complaints as long it's standing.* I agreed and told them I could have it cut down and removed by church time Wednesday. We had voted earlier to remove the tree in conjunction with the approval of the plan to construct the new sanctuary. They assured me of their support, and the tree was gone by Wednesday.

My middle-aged deacon was really upset with some of the things that had been said to me and the way they had been said. He felt that something should be done to address it. I agreed and told them I wanted to think about the matter for a few days and allow time for the matter and emotions to settle down a bit.

Wednesday evening came. The tree had been removed on Monday. It was cut close to the ground and one had to look close to know that a tree had been there. I talked with my children's classes' director and told him I wanted him to dismiss all classes 30 minutes early and have everyone come to auditorium.

I taught a Bible Study in the main auditorium on Wednesday evenings. I concluded my study for the evening about 30 minutes early and asked folks to sit quietly until the rest of the church arrived in the auditorium. You could have heard a pin drop! Later people told me they thought I was going to resign. That is not what took place.

Once all classes, teachers and children arrived, I read a prepared statement. I began by mentioning the obvious that the Dogwood tree was no longer in the front yard. I reminded them of the vote to remove the tree and the reason why it was to be removed. I did not dwell long by doing a postmortem on the tree.

I recounted the unkind things that had been said on Sunday morning and the unchristian way in which they had been said. I reminded them that I had feelings and that our relationship as pastor and church and church member with church member was more important than a tree that had been under a death sentence. I finished the statement by saying. *I do not want to hear that Dogwood tree ever mentioned again*! Some who were angry when they came in that evening apologized in tears on their way out the door.

Why mention this story? A wise leader does his best to deflect and shield those he leads. I could have responded it was not my fault and pointed the finger at the man who had actually caused me so much grief.

If we expect those we lead to be loyal to us, then they must feel confident that we will be loyal to them. There are a number of things which help engender loyalty. There are three important ones that top the list.

- The first is learning to deflect blame away from those you lead. Does that mean they should not be held accountable for their mistakes? Absolutely not! They should and must be held responsible for their actions, performance, and position-related shortcomings. That accountability must be confined to the leader and the person being led. This process was covered in detail in a previous chapter.

When problems arise publically, it is important to protect those you lead. Publically placing blame may lead to embarrassment, hurt feelings, low morale, and a feeling of being alone and abandoned to the individual.

Using the word *WE* when publically

addressing shortcomings shield the individual. It also keeps the focus where it should be, on the problem at hand. By saying something like; *we made a mistake and we are taking steps to correct it* lets those you lead know you have their backs. They understand that you appreciate them not only for the good things they do but also when they mess up you still are there for them and they are safe within the group.

Another good statement is; *this area is under my responsibilities and I take full responsibility for the mistake.* Leaders who feel they must always blame others for mistakes demonstrate feelings of inadequacy. Leaders should be willing to share the blames along with those they lead. They will earn their respect and also their loyalty. You may need the support of those people when the chips are down later.

- A second important thing to remember is always give

credit for successes to those you lead. Remember that as a leader, you are only as good as those who work with you. It's their gifts, talents, and hard work that are the bedrock of any organization. The leader may carry the burden of directing the organization, but it's on the shoulders of those that follow him who carry the load of the work, which ultimately determines success or failure.

Good leaders understand that employees and volunteer workers need recognition and praise. They need to feel they are needed, appreciated and that their labor is worthwhile. Recognizing and praising publically - individuals, employees, departments, committees, boards, etc. for their work will provide some of that needed recognition.

Occasionally do something special for them. Without letting anyone know ahead of time, declare it Ice Cream Day. Grab someone to help you and make a Dairy Queen run. Send the word out that there is a special meeting, and require everyone to attend. When they arrive, tell the employees that you just want them to know that you appreciate them and to enjoy the ice cream. Once in a while, when you go out of town, bring back small gifts. Be creative but be determined to find ways to recognize and praise those who make you successful.

- A third thing to remember is to let others recognize and praise you and your leadership. If you treat them with respect and appreciate and praise them, they will follow wherever you lead.

By the way, when I was loading up boxes from my office, while packing to move, I found a picture the Dogwood Tree someone had laid on my desk earlier that day. I keep it in my desk drawer to remind me of that tough day and to remember well the things I learned from it.

R
M
H

STUDY GUIDE

Chapter 8 It's Not My Fault

1. Leaders should do their best to _________ and _________ those they lead.

2. The leader who wants others to be __________ to him must make them feel confident that he will be __________ to them.

3. There are at least ___________ important things which help engender loyalty.

4. The first is learning to ____________ blame _________ from those being led.

5. Why is it especially important for the leader to protect those whom he leads when public problems arise?

____

____

6. Using the word ____ when publically addressing issues shields the individual.

7. Leaders who constantly blame others ____________ feeling of ___________.

8. By sharing the blame leaders will earn the _________ and __________ of those they lead.

9. Giving ___________ for success to those being led is the second important thing to remember in building loyalty.

10. Leaders should remember that they are ______ as good as those who ______ with them.

11. Their talents, gifts and hard work are the

____________ of the organization.

12. Good leaders understand that workers need ____________ and ___________.

13. Workers want to feel ____________, _____________ and that their labor is ______________.

14. The leader should ____ others recognize and ________ him.

R
M
H

Chapter 9

I Take it Back

Choose Words Wisely

I take it back.

One should think before he speaks. I was getting my feet wet in my first church. I'd barely finished my second month as pastor and was out of town participating in wedding festivities 500 miles away. The voice on the other end began to break, as the words just seemed to hang in the air around me. A terrible tragedy had just occurred in one of my church families.

I'd had the privilege of leading a lady to the Lord shortly after arriving as pastor. She had three of the cutest little girls you've ever seen. Her husband was unsaved and but was a good, decent, hard-working man. The voice on the other end gave me the details of what had happened.

The family's backyard was surrounded by a chain link fence which provided a safe environment for the girls. The four-year-old accidently stepped on a bee and was stung. Mom swept her up on her arms and took her inside to tend the wound. She told the seven-year-old she would only be gone a minute and to watch the 18-month-old until she could remove the stinger and put some medicine on the wound.

She returned a few minutes later and to her horror, found the 18-month-old face down in the small swimming pool. A neighbor came running to the mother's screams of horror. He applied CPR but could not revive the child.

The call was to not only inform me of the terrible accident which had happened but to let me know the family wanted me to preach the funeral. This would not only be my first child funeral but also my first funeral period!

Fast forward six months later. The husband has accepted the Lord but the grieving process had taken its toll. The marriage was in trouble, and the couple turned to me for counseling.

I loved this family with a pastor's heart and wanted to do all I could to help them. I met with them together and separately; my wife with me when I met with the lady. After a few sessions, the problem became apparent.

They both were hurting deeply from the loss of their daughter. They were directing that hurt towards each other. Instead of pulling and grieving together they were coming apart. The hurt resulted in numerous arguments that turned into verbal attacks on each other.

In the heat of one argument, the husband yelled at his wife *you killed my baby.* He later apologized and told her didn't mean it. But the damage had been done.

He authenticated the terrible guilt she was already feeling. She blamed herself for something that was just a terrible accident. He was sorry for what he said but she never forgot it or got over it. The couple stayed together a few more years but I received word after moving to a new pastorate in another city, that they had divorced.

Why would I relate such a sad story and what does it have to do with this chapter? Words do matter. One might be sorry for something said, but keep in mind that once said it can never be taken back. It may also never be forgotten. Temper and emotional responses must be checked at the door of leadership. Many times it is not what you say but how you say it.

Employees or volunteer workers should never be disciplined or corrected in front of others. Words spoken in that setting sting, embarrass, demoralize, and leave a bad taste in the mouths of the hearers. The leader may quickly lay the incident to rest in his mind and feel that the matter has been taken care and is over. But the person on the receiving may never forget it.

Temperament and demeanor also convey messages. Carrying oneself in a way, which shows anger when imparting correction or instruction, leaves a lasting negative impression to those on the receiving end.

Voice inflection and *tone* are also important. Raising one's voice does not make you right or more powerful. Those whom you are leading probably will not remember a week from now what you said but they may never forget the way you said it. If you raise your voice, yell, or scream, you will spend credibility at an accelerated rate and you may never be able to recoup it.

It is normally better to *act* than to *react.* Apply that age old advice we learned in elementary school about crossing the street. Stop.... Look..... And Listen. When we became agitated, angry, or upset with those we are leading, we should stop, back off, and hold our tongues. We should choose carefully what we are going to say, when to say it, and where it should be said.

Always remember that others may never forget what you say. *You Killed My Baby!* I'll never forget those words and I did not hear them personally the day they were spoken. But they have echoed in my mind and through the decades and two generations of family members.

STUDY GUIDE

Chapter 9 I Take it Back

1. Once something is ________ it can never be ________ ______ and it may never be ____________.

2. ________ and _________ should be checked at the door of leadership.

3. Many times it's not what the leader _____ but how he _____ it that matters.

4. Workers should never be _____________ or ___________ in front of others. Why? ______________________________________ ______________________________________

____

____

5. ______________ and ______________ convey messages.

6. ________ ____________ and tone are also important. Why? _____________

____

____

____

7. Normally it is better to ________ than to react.

8. The leader should follow the elementary school admonition of for crossing the street. He should ________, ________ and _________ before speaking.

9. When the leader becomes agitated, angry, or upset with those he leads, he should ______, __________ and hold _____ _________.

10. Leaders should choose carefully ________they will say, ________ to say it and _________ it should be _________.

11. The leader should always remember that others man never ________ what he said.

R
M
H

Chapter 10

Get'er Done

Use Time Wisely

Get'er Done!

My junior year in high school provided the opportunity to choose one elective class in addition to the required courses for graduation. My plans were to eventually go into business, so I enrolled in a one-semester course titled

Personal Typing. I thought the class might help me later on with personal and business-related correspondence, etc. That was before the days of the Internet and email. I never realized then how much that small decision would benefit me throughout the rest of my life.

Those who are inducted into the Armed Forces of the United States undergo a battery of tests to determine their skills and where they may be of most benefit to the military. I could type almost 50 words a minute and they determined I would be more valuable working in an office rather than in a foxhole.

I eventually ended up with my own office with a wide range of responsibilities assigned to me. This would become a pattern for many years to come. The responsibilities seemed to increase along with the numbers of people who I was directly or indirectly responsible for overseeing. Increased responsibility demands wise use of the leader's time.

There are more time robbers leaders

must avoid now than at any time in history. With the Internet, smart phones, email, Facebook, Twitter, etc., leaders must be proactive if they are going to accomplish the tasks their leadership roles demand.

If the leader does not develop an effective approach to wisely using his time he will find himself late for appointments, late with projects, throwing things together at the last minute, burning the midnight oil, wasting time, under constant stress, and a multitude of other things.

I developed an approach to manage time during my early years of ministry. It has served me well and hopefully it will provide insight that may help other leaders as they work to maximize their time and use it more effectively.

Accomplish Twice as Much This Year

The observations on ways for leaders to use time wisely and become more effective will be divided into five parts. Each part will be built upon the previous one(s). The parts are as follows: Part 1′ Getting things done in a lifetime, Part 2′ Getting things done in the next 12 Months, Part 3′ Getting things done in the next month, Part 4′ Getting things done this week and Part 5′ Getting things done today.

- Part 1 – ***Getting things done in a lifetime***. Each person should develop lifelong goals. The years come and go and life moves much more quickly than we are aware of. Setting lifelong goals, helps the leader feel a sense of purpose and can be effective in guiding his present and future decisions.

My four lifelong goals are framed by my Christian faith and love for family. I developed these goals at about age 20 and before the first of my two children was born and these goals are still lifelong goals today. The most important lifelong goal was to live a life of honor, integrity, and purity in order to *glorify the God that I serve*.

The second lifelong goal was to *go to Heaven*. They may seem trivial too some people, but I believe that there is life after death and the moment we leave this world we end up in another one. I wanted to make sure I ended up in the right one.

The third lifelong goal was to *build a close and loving family*. The wise leader will realize early that his family must come before his work. If he fails to learn this early, he will find out at some point that success on the job can never take the place of a warm and loving family. Close families don't just happen. They require hard work and the investment of time, talent, and treasure. The last thing I wanted was to become successful professionally, only to down the line lose my wife and/or children in the process.

The fourth lifelong goal was to be used by the Lord to *make a difference in this world*. I committed early to a lifetime of serving others. I wanted to make sure I never allowed myself to become involved in anything that might cause me to be disqualified from serving others.

What must we do in order to accomplish these lifelong goals?

1. Pray (Seek God's wisdom in all your decisions and planning.)
2. Establish Specific Objects (Determine what you hope to do.)
3. Prioritize Your Objectives (Determine the order of importance.)
4. Develop Steps necessary to accomplish your objectives. (Determine how you will accomplish each objective.)
5. Create a time line for the next 12 months. (Assign steps to be taken month by month.)
6. Set Realistic Goals for the upcoming month.

7. Plan your Schedule for the next week.
8. Stick to your schedule for today.

- Part 2 – ***Getting things done in the next 12 months***. How should the leader plan affectively for the next year? Trying to get one's arms around 365 days of scheduling might seem like a daunting task on the surface, but it can be done. The following helped me greatly and can be of help to most leaders;
    - *Make a list of all the important events* and the dates that will take place in the next 12 months.

    - *Establish and prioritize Objectives.*(Determine what you hope to do.)
        - Make a list of major projects you hope to do

this year. (This should be small and realistic.)

- Number each in order of importance.

- *Develop Steps necessary to accomplish each objective.*
  - Define the purpose of each project. (One project at a time.)
  - Determine resources that will be needed. (Personal, material, finances, etc.)
  - Delegate specific responsibilities to volunteer or paid staff. (If appropriate.)
  - Develop a 12-month timeline showing due dates for project steps.

- Part 3 – ***Getting things done next month***. The coming month's schedule will be impacted by what the leader was able to accomplish this past month. How do you determine what needs to be done next month? Four things listed below may be helpful for the leader to remember;

- Review the project deadlines which were assigned to this coming month at the beginning of the year.
- Review projects, which were assigned to be accomplished last month and if necessary, reassign them to be done this coming month.
- Make a list of additional items that must be done this coming month.
- Assign specific days in which these tasks should be worked on.

- Part 4 – ***Getting things done this week***. We've looked at how to schedule, how to accomplish lifelong goals, goals for the next 12 months and goals for next month. All five parts are valuable and can benefit the leader. We now get down to where the rubber really meets the road. The weekly schedule will make or break the leader in getting things done.

There are three important categories into which every event this coming week will fall. These are: 1. Things that must be done this week ***at a certain time***. 2. Things which must be done this week but ***at no certain time***.

3. Things I would like to do ***if I get the time***. Below are scheduling steps incorporating those three categories which can be of tremendous help to the leader in planning his weekly schedule.

1. Make a list of **things that must be done this week at certain times.**
    - Drop kids at school.
    - Sunday morning church.

- Annual physical
- Meeting with various managers.
- Days off
- Pick kids up from school

2. Now **transfer each event** from the list to corresponding times on whatever you use to keep your schedule (Outlook, desk calendar, etc.) Be sure to block off sufficient time for each task.)
3. You have just **prioritized your schedule** for the week placing priority on the things that must get done and reserved times for each of them to get done.
4. Make a list of things that **must be done but at no certain time**.
    - Prepare PowerPoint presentation.
    - Check email.

- Answer phone calls.
- Put car in the shop.
- Cut the grass.
- Study for Sunday
- Take wife to lunch.

5. Look through the list and **pick out the most important thing**, choose a time on your schedule, transfer it over to your schedule, and then cross it off the list.
6. Repeat this until **all *have- to-get-done*** items are been placed on your schedule.
7. Make a list of things **you'd like to do if you get the time**.
   - Go by Bass Pro Shop.
   - Play Golf.
   - Visit a bookstore.
8. Pick out the most important thing you'd like to do. Check the available times remaining on

your schedule and reserve the time for this event.

9. Transfer the remaining things you'd like to do one at a time until you've crossed all of them off your list.
10. Congratulations, you've successfully scheduled all the events that must be done this week and also worked some things you'd like to do.

- Part 5 – ***Getting things done today***. Sticking as closely to the schedule you've worked is key. The unexpected comes up from time to time, but the wise leader should plan his work and then work the plan.

The wise Leader will evaluate regularly how well he is using his time. Surfing the web, checking Facebook every ten minutes, having an automatic email notification on phone and/or computer, computer games, etc. can and will rob the leader of his time.

Do you find yourself late with appointments or projects or wasting a lot of time? Do you tend to throw things together at the last minute? You know you are not putting as much time as you should into study, writing, exercise, taking care of personal finances, and more. Do you find it difficult to get things done that you know must be done because you are constantly running short on time? Do you feel overwhelmed with seemingly no way to get it all done?

Good News – You can get most if not all of it done. You'll be surprised what can be accomplished with wise planning and proper scheduling.

STUDY GUIDE

Chapter 10 "Get'er" done!

1. Increased responsibility _________ wise use of the leader's time.

2. Leaders must be ___________ if they expect to complete the tasks their roles demand.

3. Setting _________ goals can be effective in guiding the leader's present and future decisions.

4. What are four lifetime goals suggested by the author.

   a. ________________________________

b. ____________________________________

c. ____________________________________

d. ____________________________________

5. What eight things will aid in the leader accomplishing these goals.

   a.____

   b. ____________________________________

   c. _____________________________________

   d. _____________________________________

   e. _____________________________________

   f. ___________________________________

   g. ___________________________________

h. ______________________________

6. How can the leaders get things done over the next 12 months?

   a. Make a list of ________ _____ and the dates they will take place.

   b. Establish __________ and ______.

   c. Develop _________ necessary to ___________ each objective.

7. How can leaders get things done over the next month?

   a. Review the ________ _______ which were assigned to this coming month at the beginning of the year.

b. Review projects which were assigned to be accomplished ____ ______ and if necessary, ________them to be done this coming month.

c. Make a list of ____________ ________ that must be done this coming month.

d. Assign __________ ______ in which these tasks should be worked on.

8. What are 10 things leaders can do to help them get things done this week? (in order)

a. Make a list of things that should be done at __________ _____.

b. ____________ each event on the list to corresponding times on whatever the leader uses to keep his schedule.

c. ___________ your schedule for the week.

d. Make a list of things that should be done but at _________ ____ ________.

e. Look through the list and pick out the most __________ _____, _________a time on the leader's schedule, _________ it over to his schedule and then _______it off the list.

f. This should be ____________ until all the items which have to be done are scheduled.

g. Make a list of things you'd ______ __ __ if you get the time.

h. The leaders should pick out the _____ __________ thing he'd like to do. Check the ___________ times remaining on his schedule and ____________the time for this event

i. Transfer the ___________ ________ you'd like to do one at a time until you've _________ all of them off your list.

j. The leader has successfully ____________ all the events that must be done _______ _____ and also worked in some things he'd like _____ ________.

9. How can leaders get things done today?

____

____

____

____

10. The wise leader will __________ __________ how well he is using his time.

11. Leaders may be surprised with what can be accomplished with ________ planning and __________ scheduling.

R
M
H

Chapter 11

Taking Care of Business

Conducting Business Meetings

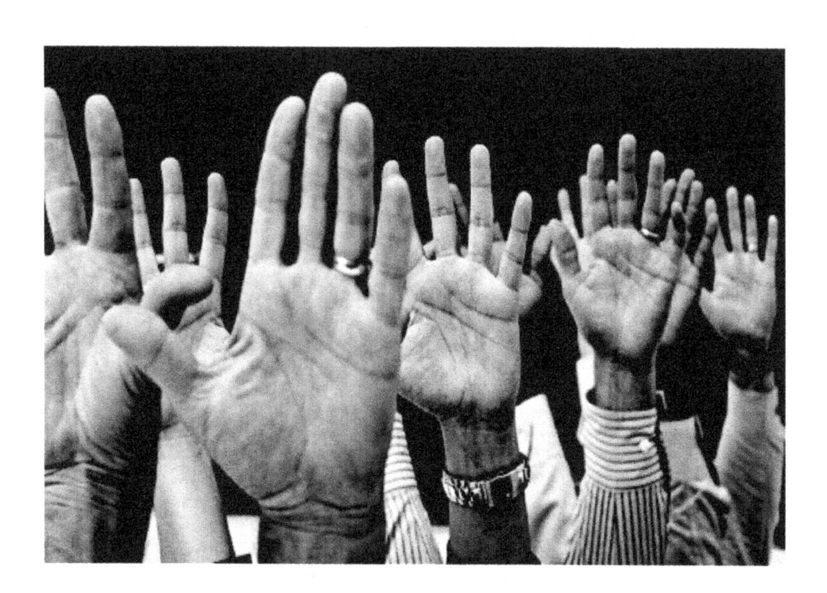

Taking Care of Business.

For some, the very mention of the term *business meeting* sends a shiver up the spine, much like being reminded of an upcoming root canal. Business meetings create dread, anxiety, even fear—especially when difficult issues must be addressed. Yet business meetings, whether at the local, district, state, or national levels are necessary.

While we may never experience a sense of euphoria about an upcoming business meeting, we can defeat the dread and make meetings run more smoothly and successfully by considering the following suggestions:

- **Be punctual.** Start the meeting on time. This sets the tone for the meeting and demonstrates respect for those in attendance.

- **Be prepared.** Advance preparation helps the meeting stay focused and saves time. Good preparation includes an agenda, listing each item to be addressed. (Note the example at the end of the chapter.)

- **Be productive.** The following helpful hints—common sense, really—will help you get the most from your meeting. Ask that all discussion, comments, and questions be directed to the moderator. (This will help keep order and keep differences of opinion from getting out of hand.) Always get a motion and second on the floor before allowing discussion. This will help keep the discussion from wandering and wasting time. A motion is not a motion until the moderator recognizes it, repeats it, and asks for a second. After a motion and second, allow ample time for discussion but don't allow the debate to drag on indefinitely.

Know Your Motions

Three types of motions generally arise in business meetings: *main motions, incidental motions*, and *motions to bring a question back to the assembly*. The list below cites common motions that arise in business meetings:

Main Motions

The motions below are ordered by priority. Any

motion below can be made, and is in order, if it appears higher on the list than the one already made below it.

- **Motion to adjourn:** Everyone enjoys this motion because it signals an end to the meeting. However, the motion to adjourn cannot interrupt a person speaking, requires a second, is not debatable, cannot be amended and requires a majority vote.
- **Motion to table (or lay on the table):** Defers an item of business to another time. It must meet the following requirements: It cannot interrupt a person speaking, requires a second, is not debatable, cannot be amended, and requires a majority vote. Note: Outside the United States, to table a motion means you make the item available for consideration.

- **Motion for previous question:** Calls for an end to discussion. It cannot interrupt a person speaking, requires a second, is not debatable, cannot be amended, and requires a two-thirds majority.

- **Motion to postpone:** Delays the action as determined by the body. It cannot interrupt a person speaking, requires a second, is not debatable, cannot be amended, and requires a majority vote.

- **Motion to refer the matter to a committee:** Defers the item of business to a smaller subsection of the voting body. A committee is often used when more research is required or details need to be handled outside of a public forum. It cannot interrupt a person speaking, requires a second, is not debatable, cannot be amended, and requires a majority vote.

- **Motion to amend:** Adds to or alters an existing motion to make it more acceptable to the voting body, usually based on discussion. It cannot interrupt a person speaking, requires a second, is debatable, can be amended once, and requires a majority vote.

- **Motion to postpone indefinitely:** This motion effectively kills the item of business. It cannot interrupt a person speaking, requires a second, is not debatable, cannot be amended, and requires a majority vote.

Incidental Motions (No order of priority and dealt with immediately.)

- **Point of order:** Indicates a breach of protocol. Can interrupt someone speaking, does not require a second, is not debatable, cannot be amended, no vote is taken, and the moderator decides the validity of the point.

- **Appeal the decision of the chair:** Occurs when an individual does not agree with the ruling of the moderator. The motion may interrupt someone speaking, requires a second, is debatable, cannot be amended, and requires a majority vote to overrule the moderator's decision.

- **Motion to suspend the rules:** Permits the voting body to supersede the established rules. The motion cannot interrupt someone speaking, requires a second, is not debatable, cannot be amended, and requires a two-thirds vote.

- **Objection to the consideration of a question:** Prevents an embarrassing or manipulative question from public forum. The motion can interrupt a person speaking, does not need a second, is not debatable, cannot be amended, and requires a two-thirds vote.

Motions to Return a Previous Motion

- **Remove from the table:** Brings back a motion tabled earlier. The motion cannot interrupt a person speaking, requires a second, is not debatable, cannot be amended, and requires a majority vote.

- **Rescind a previous motion:** Reverses an action upon which the voting body has already agreed. It cannot interrupt a person speaking, must be made by a person who voted for the previously adopted motion, requires a second, is debatable, can be amended, and requires a majority vote providing the body has been notified ahead of time.

(You may want to keep a copy of these motions with you as a reference when moderating business meetings.)

Smooth business meetings will help organizations accomplish their missions and set a course for future success. Following these simple suggestions should make business meetings productive and run more smoothly. They will relieve some stress, reduce anxiety, and save you money on Rolaids or Maalox!

Simple Meeting Agenda

1. Call the meeting to order.
2. Recognize and "seat" the delegates (have them stand).
- Standing delegates
- Elected delegates
3. Recognize the clerk or secretary for the written record of the
previous meeting's proceedings (minutes).
- Ask for a motion* and second to receive the report.
- Ask for questions or discussion.
- Approve the minutes.
4. Recognize the treasurer to give the financial report.
- Ask for a motion* and second to receive the report.

- Ask for questions or discussion.
- Approve the minutes.

5. Introduce Board and Committee reports.

- Ask for a motion* and second to receive each report.
- Ask for questions or discussion.
- Approve the minutes.

6. Review any unfinished business from previous meetings (old business).
7. Ask if there is any new business to come before the body.
8. When you've covered your last item, ask for a motion to adjourn.

* If minutes and reports are printed and distributed, there may be no need to
read them aloud. Ask for additions or corrections. If none are required, approve
the minutes as written. No motion is needed.

STUDY GUIDE

Chapter 11 Taking Care of Business

1. What three suggestions can make business meetings run more smoothly and successful?
    a. ____________________
    b. ____________________
    c. ____________________

2. What are three types of motions which generally arise at business meetings?
    a. ____________________
    b. ____________________
    c. ____________________

3. List the main motions in order of priority.

    ____

____

____

____

4. List the incidental motions – they have no order of __________ and are dealt with ______________.

____

____

____

5. What are the motions involving returning to a return to a previous motion?

   a. ___________________________________

   b. ___________________________________

Chapter 12

If I had Known then

Second Guessing Past Decisions

The author enjoys dawning his coveralls and working on his old 1998 Chevy Silverado 4X4 pickup truck in his shop out back.

If I'd only known then....

I arrived at Fort Leonard Wood, Missouri, my permanent duty station. My wife and six-week-old daughter were soon able to join me. After living in a small mobile home for about three months, I was able to secure a three-bedroom apartment in an on-post housing complex. We were thrilled to have that much room. My enlisted man's salary was very meager, but we had what we needed and enjoyed our life in the military.

My father was a gifted man who could fix almost anything. I believe I inherited some of that from him. That can be a great blessing but a curse at times as well. Before electronic ignition and 100,000-mile intervals between tune-ups, there were things called *points* and *spark plugs* which had to be changed on your car about once per year. My father had taught me how to change those spark plugs and points.

I will not bore you with the details and in workings of the automobile gasoline combustion engine, but I will tell you a true story that taught me a great lesson. I purchased new spark plugs and points at a local auto parts store and made plans to change them the next day.

I raised the car hood laid out all the parts on the fender and proceeded. The process of removing the old spark plugs and installing the new ones went fairly quickly and was uneventful. Now came time for the points.

When I loosened the screw that held them in place, the screw accidently dropped down the inside shaft of the distributor. The points came with an extra screw so I didn't think much about it. I installed the new points, set the proper gap to make them open and close at the correct intervals and tightened everything down.

Everything looked good. The only thing left was to start the engine. When the key turned, the ignition engaged the starter and then a loud bang came from the engine. Now a loud bang from your car engine is never a good thing.

I had no idea what had happened, but I had a bad feeling that it had something to do with those points and that little screw that had dropped down inside. Over and over again I tried to start the car. It didn't even sound like it wanted to start.

I had no idea what to do. I was several hundreds of miles from home on a military post with virtually no extra money to spend, and our only means of transportation disabled. I felt like crying, but we all know *grown men don't cry.*

We'd become good friends with our next door neighbors. We watched their little girl from time to time and they watched ours. The Sergeant heard the repeated attempts and failures to start the engine. I was a little embarrassed and relieved at the same time when I saw him walk through his front door, down the steps and to my car.

I stepped out of the car and heard his question; *won't she start?* I told him no and he asked me to turn it over again. He did something under the hood and then told me to turn the key off. The motor wasn't getting any fire he said. Then he asked me what had happened. I explained that I had changed the plugs and points and accidently dropped a screw down inside the distributor. He then said; *man you've got a problem.*

My fears were now being realized. He removed the bolt that held the distributor in place on top of the engine and pulled the distributer from the motor. He showed me the broken shaft on the bottom of the distributer. The loud bang I heard was that huge V-8 motor had in a split second twisted off the bottom of the distributor shaft. Part of the broken shaft remained lodged in the engine and the only way to reach it was through a hole the size of the bottom of a Pepsi can.

I was very fortunate that my neighbor's

job was a mechanic in the Motor pool (the Army's version of a vehicle repair shop). He used a wire coat hanger to dislodge the broken piece and a magnet retrieved it through the hole on top of the motor. He drove me to a junk yard and I bought a used distributor which came from a wrecked car, and together we installed the used distributor.

The car started, and the problem was solved.

There were several lessons learned though this troubling experience. The first one is obvious. Be careful when you drop your screws. A second lesson is when you drop one be sure you know what you are doing before you move forward. BOY, IF I'D ONLY KNOWN THEN WHAT I KNOW NOW, I WOULD HAVE MADE A DIFFERENT DESION.

There is at least one more lesson that can be learned from this episode. Fretting over past decisions is a waste of time. I wish I had not turned the key and tried to start the car while the screw was still lodged in the distributor. I did not know that it would cause as much damage as it did. If I'd known then what I know now, I would have consulted my neighbor after I'd dropped the screw and before I made such a mess of things.

Leading is not easy and one cannot change the past or live in the future. Decision making is a process. One should become as knowledgeable as possible on the matter at hand. He should give careful thought to what might be gained or lost and how the decision might impact the people and relationships involved. He should determine a sense of direction. Then he should make the decision.

Decisions must be based on the information available at the moment. There is no other way to do it. You will not have tomorrow's information until tomorrow arrives.

What about yesterday's decisions? One

should not second guess past decisions because more information becomes available later. We make decisions based on what we know now. If we'd known more before, we might have made a different decision. We go with what we know. Dwelling on past decisions is a waste of energy.

Some past decisions may be changed or corrected as more information becomes available. There is nothing wrong with veering to the right or left or even doing an about-face on a past decision. Just because an adjustment can or should be made is no reason to beat yourself up over the original decision. Leaders are not clairvoyant (somebody who is supposedly able to perceive things that are usually beyond the range of human senses). They can learn from the past, make decisions in the present, and make adjustments in the future.

STUDY GUIDE

Chapter 12 If I'd Only Known Then

1. __________ over past decisions is a __________ of time.
2. ___________ is not easy.
3. The leader should remember that he cannot _________ the past or ________ in the future.
4. Leaders should gain as much ______________ as possible about the matter at hand.
5. Leaders should give careful thought to what might be _____________ and what might be ___________ and how decisions may ___________ the people and relationships involved.
6. Leaders should ___________ a sense of direction and then __________ the decision.

7. Decisions must be __________ on the ____________ available at the moment.
8. Leaders should not _________ ________ past decisions because more information becomes available later.
9. Leaders must make decisions based on what they ___________.
10. ___________ on past decisions is a waste of ___________.
11. Past decisions may be _________ or ___________ if more information becomes available.
12. Leaders can _________ from the past, _______ ________ in the present and _________ ______________ in the future.

Study Guide Answers

Chapter 1 Leading from the Grease Trap

1. A. The employees and manager were a team. B. The manager was willing to get his hands dirty and do the worst job.
2. Loyalty and morale.
3. Model the work ethic
4. Standards and expectations
5. Disconnect
6. Them
7. Morale, loyalty
8. he probably has not modeled well who is the boss to the employees or volunteers
9. for, with
10. Creating camaraderie and willingness to follow requires the leader to;
    a. Direction, expectations b. example, coming alongside
11. Loyal, believe

Chapter 2 Count the Cost

1. Decision, requirement
2. Guide, courses
3. What is there to be gained and what could be lost?
4. Cost, benefit
5. Benefit, cost
6. Businesslike, respect
7. Is the issue worth losing a relationship over?
8. Yes – discussion
9. Two
10. Morals, ethics, biblical principles
11. Encounter
12. Unethical, precedence
13. Proven disloyalty to you as the leader
14. Loyalty
15. Biblical principle
16. preference, choice or a simple matter of opinion

17. Compromise, not do
18. Important questions
19. Instinct, benefit
20. Creative.

Chapter 3 Aim Before Firing

1. Cautious, reading
2. Accurately
3. Who, what, when, where
4. WHAT
5. If it is a small matter and is old news, it may not be worth the time and effort to address it now. If is a recent small matter that can and should be dealt with, then knowing the WHEN is important
6. Serious matters should be dealt with sooner rather than later. Moving quickly reinforces the importance and seriousness of the matter.
7. WHO, the present situation may be connected to another situation. Knowing who is involved is essential in knowing how to handle the situation.

8. WHERE, location, took place.
9. Legal, authorities
10. Alone, work
11. Controversy

Chapter 4 I Don't Like It!

RECEIVING CRITICISM

1. Listen
2. Criticism, nothing, something.
3. a. Listen to it, b. Look at it, c. Learn from it, d. Live above it.
4. Past confrontations or disagreements. Maybe because they are on the other side of an issue. Maybe it is just a matter of personality conflicts.
5. You may miss the message.
6. Merit, a. Are the facts accurate? b. Is the criticism valid? c. Is there a hidden agenda?
7. Personal pride, stubbornness

8. Improved, corrected
9. Actions, corrections, adjustments
10. Plan, make
11. After listening to and looking at criticism and finding it without merit, determine that he will simply *live above it*. Keep doing what he's been doing.

GIVING CRITICISM

1. Give, manner
2. Time, manner
3. Offer, solutions

FINAL THOUGHTS

1. Please, time
2. a. Listen b. Look c. Learn d. Live
3. do, believes, path, discerned

Chapter 5 Say What?

1. Tether
2. Real, perceived

3. Schedule regular meetings with those whom one leads.
4. a. Informed b. successes, concerns, personal issues c. appreciation, concerns, instructions d. something, chest
5. Never
6. Leader's office
7. Frame
8. Door, closed
9. Door, cracked, wide open
10. This communicates to those you labor with that you want to be left alone. It also conveys a message that you are unapproachable.
11. for confidentiality, times of personal study, private phone calls, when deadlines are pressing
12. Area, responsibility
13. It lets them know that the leader knows where they labor and what they do. It also communicates that what they do is important.

14. a. Face to Face b. Email c. Phone d. Texting

FINAL THOUGHTS

1. More, communicate
2. Unsaid. Discourage
3. Little, suspicion, much
4. Cannot
5. Conduit, communication

Chapter 6 A Visit with the Sergeant Major

1. Delegate
2. People, volunteers
3. Careful selection of those workers the leader surrounds himself with.
4. Better, areas
5. LOYALTY
6. Credibility, good name
7. Define the parameters
8. Do their work
9. Handing, hanging

10. Creativity, morale
11. Lifeline, ball
12. Expecting results
13. Expect, inspect
14. Inspected
15. Completion, accountable
16. a. What b. Who c. When d. When
17. Praise, recognition
18. Costs, very little
19. Dividends, projects

Chapter 7 The Positive/Negative Approach

1. Meet expectations
2. Shortcomings, repeated offenses
3. Email, text, telephone
4. Misunderstood, print
5. Facial expression, crossed arms and legs, nervous shifting around in the chair, lack of eye contact, etc. may indicate the true manner in which the person is receiving

what is being sent their way. The leader's body language may also convey to the person on the receiving the leader's sincerity, displeasure.

6. The Office, The setting is more private and confidential, The person will more readily accept correction or criticism in the office.
7. It is a symbol of the leader's position and authority. Sitting behind the desk when admonishing or correcting, will reinforce the roles and remind the person on the receiving end of his personal accountability.
8. What, how
9. Genuine appreciation - Doing this before bringing up the negative matter frames the conversation in a positive context.
10. Calling the person by name and saying something like; Bill, there is something we need to talk about. Then proceed to share the issue at hand.
11. Jot, reminder

12. Questions, feelings, side
13. Plan, problem
14. What do you think we should do now?
15. Rise from the office chair, come around the desk. Shake hands with the individual and conclude the meeting looking him in the eye and letting him know he is appreciated and how important his service is to the church or organization.
16. It will often leave a good taste in their mouths and a positive frame of mind.
17. Closing the door quickly may send a wrong signal that the leader is glad to get rid of them. By waiting it may signal to them that both they and their time are important to the leader.
18. Leading, building
19. Relationships, inspiring
20. This will hinder the relationship. This could negatively impact the church

or organization because matters which need joint input, strategy and effort may unintentionally be sacrificed.

Chapter 8 It's Not My Fault

1. Deflect, shield
2. Loyal, loyal
3. Three
4. Deflect, away
5. Publically placing blame may lead to embarrassment, hurt feelings, low morale and a feeling of being alone and abandoned to the individual.
6. WE
7. Demonstrate, inadequacy
8. Respect, loyalty
9. Credit
10. Only, work
11. Bedrock
12. Recognition, praise
13. Needed, appreciated, worthwhile
14. Let, praise

Chapter 9 I Take it Back

1. Said, back
2. Temper, emotional
3. What, says
4. Disciplined, corrected - Words spoken in that setting sting, embarrass, demoralize, and leave a bad taste in the mouths of the hearer. The person on the receiving may never forget it.
5. Temperament, demeanor
6. Voice inflection - If you raise your voice, yell or scream, you will spend credibility at an accelerated rate and you may never be able to recoup it.
7. Act
8. Stop, look, listen
9. Stop, back off, hold his tongue
10. What, when, where, said
11. Forget

Chapter 10 "Get'er" done!

1. Demands
2. Proactive

3. Lifelong
4. Life-Long Goals
    a. Live a life of honor, integrity, and purity in order to glorify the God I serve.
    b. God to Heaven one day.
    c. Build a close and loving family.
    d. Be used by the Lord to make a difference in this world.
5. Eight aids to help accomplish lifelong goals.
    a. Pray b. Establish Objectives c. Prioritize Objectives d. Develop steps to accomplish objectives. e. Create a 12-month timeline f. Set Goals g. Plan schedule for the next week. h. Stick to the schedule today.
6. Getting things done over the next 12 months.
    a. Important events b. Establish, prioritize c. Steps, accomplish
7. Getting things done over the next month.

   a. Project deadlines b. last month, reassign c. additional items d. specific days.
8. 10 things leaders can do to get things done in a week.
   a. a certain time b. Transfer c. Prioritize d. no set time e. the important time, transfer, cross f. Repeated g. like to do h. most important thing. available times, reserve i. remaining things, crossed j. scheduled, this week, to do.
9. Sticking as closely to the schedule you've worked is key.
10. Evaluate regularly
11. Wise, proper

Chapter 11 Taking Care of Business

1. Be punctual, Be prepared, Be productive.
2. Main motions, Incidental motions, Motions to return to a previous motion
3. Adjourn, Lay on the Table, Previous Question, Postpone, Refer to a

Committee, Amend, Postpone Indefinitely

4. Priority – Point of Order, Appeal the decision of the chair, Suspend the rules, Objection to Consideration of the Question
5. Remove from the table, Rescind a previous motion,

Chapter 12 If I'd Only Known Then

1. Dwelling, waste
2. Leading
3. Change, live
4. Knowledge
5. Gained, lost, impact
6. Determine, make
7. Based, information
8. Second guess
9. Know
10. Dwelling, time
11. Changed, corrected
12. Learn, make decisions, make adjustments

R
M
H

Roy Harris Ministries

began in 2007 to help and encourage pastors, churches, Christian educators, and Christian businesses.

Roy Harris Ministries has grown into a multi-dimensional outreach ministry, including but not limited to:

Living Beyond Grief Conferences
Pastor/Staff Leadership Conferences
Church Renewal Conferences
Church Evangelism Conferences
Couples Retreats
Men's Retreats
Family Enrichment Days
Traditional Church Revival Meetings

Dr. Harris is in high demand as Conference and Retreat Speaker. He has spoken in 38 American States, Europe, Israel and Africa ministering in over 400 business organizations, schools, colleges and churches.

Check the web @ www.royharris.info for more information on ways Roy might be of help to you, your church, school, or business. *Dr. Harris'* contact information:

roy@royharris.info
(615-351-1425)
906 Castle Heights Ave
Lebanon, TN 37087

Another book by Roy for those providing care to the terminally ill. For three years Roy provided loving care for his terminally ill wife Diana until her death. He wrote **Caring for the Caregiver** to encourage and help those who provide care to terminally ill loved ones and also to help others better understand how to encourage and help caregivers.

What others are saying...

"As a caregiver myself (my wife has MS), I was moved, encouraged, helped, comforted, challenged, and blessed. You will be, too." **Robert Morgan,** Senior Pastor, The Donelson Fellowship, Nashville, TN

"This book is a must for every caregiver, pastor, deacon, choir director, youth worker, health care worker, and anyone who wants to better understand how to help and encourage caregivers. Thanks Roy.... Many people will be helped and encouraged by this book." **Stan Toler,** Superintendent, Church of the Nazarene.

"If you know a caregiver, hand him a copy of this book; it's a how-to course on coming to terms with life's most difficult crises. If you become a caregiver, study this book; it's a blueprint on keeping your balance when life turns upside down. If you ever need a caregiver, read this book carefully; it will help you appreciate those who rearrange their lives to care for you." **Jack Williams**, Director of Publications, Welch College, Nashville – TN.

Copies of the book may be ordered online at **www.royharris.info** or www.amazon.com. For an autographed copy send a check for $13.99 to:

Caring for the Caregiver.
Roy Harris
906 Castle Heights Ave.
Lebanon, TN 37087

Made in the USA
Las Vegas, NV
07 January 2021

15476712R00125